I Know All
Save Myself Alone

I Know All
Save Myself Alone

The Play

Lisa Monde

Library of Congress Control Number: 2011915516
ISBN: Hardcover   978-1-4653-1035-4
             Softcover   978-1-4653-1034-7
             Ebook   978-1-4653-1036-1

To order additional copies of this book, contact:
Xlibris Corporation
1-888-795-4274
www.Xlibris.com
Orders@Xlibris.com
95532

PART 1

Scene 1

The Lifting of the *Pet-au-Diable*, Also Known as the Sow

Paris, 1452.

Late spring evening. The clock of the nearby church has just struck ten.
The Sorbonne's bell rings.

The street is plunged in darkness. Only occasional gleams coming from the windows of the nearest taverns illuminate the square in front of the hotel-mansion of Madame de Bruyeres.

A great monolith—the prehistoric stone named the *Pet-au-Diable*—stands before the mansion of Madame de Bruyeres.

Suddenly, the hurried steps and muffled voices can be heard coming from the narrow alley leading to the square.

Enter the SCHOLARS of Sorbonne.

They whisper something to one another fervently, laugh, and look around.
Some scholars carry inflamed torches; others push the squeaky old cart.
VILLON leads the procession.
GUY TABARIE, Master of Arts and VILLON's closest friend, sits in the cart.

VILLON: Hurry up, guys! Hurry up! We didn't come here to admire the stars! We have some work to do . . .

GUY TABARIE fools around.

GUY TABARIE: Hark! Listen to the poet! The stars can wait . . . The stone won't!

VILLON: Stop talking, you king of fools! Better come down and help! We'll need all our strength to move that rogue of a stone.

> GUY TABARIE gets off the cart and makes his way to the monolith.
> The SCHOLARS drag the cart toward the base of the stone.
> VILLON joins GUY TABARIE, and they both approach the stone.

> VILLON makes low bows to the *Pet-au-Diable*.

VILLON: Oh, honorable *Pet-au-Diable*! We've arrived to steal thee! This night we shall be honored to name thee—the Sow! From this moment on, your . . . existence . . . will change!

GUY TABARIE laughs.
> Suddenly he notices the flickering light of a candle in one of the mansion's windows. He strongly pulls VILLON's sleeve.

GUY TABARIE: Francois, we need to take to our heels! Now! The old witch is awake! RUN!

Meanwhile, the SCHOLARS tie the ropes round the stone and topple it over. The Sow crashes onto the cart.
> Some SCHOLARS start shouting at the top of their voices.

VILLON: What the devil is happening there with you?

He turns to see several scholars being pressed by the stone.
> The window opens, and MADAME DE BRUYERES screams.

MADAME DE BRUYERES: Help! Help! You loafers, what are you doing with my glorious palladium? THIEVES! THIEVES!

SCHOLAR 1: Palladium? Hey, that looks more like stinking feces to me!

VILLON: Hurry up, you idiots! Move the cart! Push, push!

VILLON joins the scholars and GUY TABARIE and pushes the cart with the stone as hard as he can toward the dark alley.

MADAME DE BRUYERES: Guards! Guards! Somebody! Help! Thieves! You'll be hanging on the gallows in the morning, you little bastards!

VILLON: MADAME, THE *PET-AU-DIABLE* IS NOT YOUR PROPERTY! IT'S A HISTORICAL MONUMENT OF THE CITY!

The lights start to light up in the windows of the neighboring houses.

VILLON: WE'LL FASTEN THE STONE WITH PLASTER AND IRON BARS TO ONE PLACE, AND NEITHER YOU NOR THE GUARDS WILL BE ABLE TO GET IT MOVING! SORBONNE IS INVIOLABLE!

The SCHOLARS hoot unanimously.

GUY TABARIE: VILLON, THE GUARDS!

Enter GUARDS, they scream and approach the scholars.

The SCHOLARS divide into groups. Some deal with the stone, and others grab everything they see on their way—sticks, fragments of broken glass—and throw it at the GUARDS.
    SCHOLARS tear away the signs of the taverns and beat the GUARDS with them.
    People look out of the windows.

GUARD: In the name of the king of France! Don't move!

VILLON is caught by two GUARDS. They start beating him. The fight begins.
    GUY TABARIE attacks a GUARD, helping VILLON to release himself from the rough grasp of the GUARD. The GUARD falls down to the ground, and scholars instantly surround him, leaving the cart with the stone in the middle of the street.
    SCHOLARS hit the GUARD.

SCHOLAR 1: You won't take *Pet-au-Diable* away from us! It belongs to us!

Kicks the GUARD.

SCHOLAR 2: We'll crown it with flowers, and we'll dance around it to the sound of tambourines.

    Kicks the GUARD.

SCHOLAR 3: And you will respect our Sow of the Devil!

Kicks the GUARD.

VILLON: STOP THIS! RUN! THEY CALLED FOR HELP! RUN! AND IF YOU GET CAUGHT, TELL THEM YOU WERE LED BY MICHEL MOUTON, THE BUTCHER!

VILLON runs, catches up with GUY TABARIE, and whispers to him.

VILLON: I will meet you in the Fircone tavern in Jewry Street in an hour!

VILLON and GUY TABARIE exit.
    SCHOLARS are being seized by the GUARDS.

Blackout.

Scene 2

Mad hearts of youth where wisdom's snows
Yet never fell. Alack, 'tis truth!
But they who be my fiercest foes
Don't wish me to outlive my youth.

Two weeks later.

Early spring. Matin.

The house of Guillaume de Villon close to the Saint-Benoit Church, the so-called House of the Red Door.

FRANCOIS VILLON lies, dressed, on the bed in his small room in the attic.

The light, fresh breeze plays with the leafage outside, and the timid morning sun caresses VILLON's face.

We hear footsteps on the stairs.

VILLON jumps to his feet, rushes to the writing table by the window. He randomly opens the first book that comes across and puts it in front of him on the table. He drops his head in his hands and pretends to read with concentration.

Enter FATHER GUILLAUME DE VILLON, the canon of the church and VILLON's foster father.

FATHER GUILLAUME: Francois! You are up so early! And already rush towards new knowledge.

FATHER GUILLAUME approaches VILLON and tousles his dark-brown head of hair.

VILLON turns to face FATHER GUILLAUME and smiles wearily.

VILLON: What a marvelous morning, Father!

FATHER GUILLAUME: Yes, indeed, Francois. What drove you out of your bed this morning? (*He gestures at the book.*) Who am I to blame this time?

VILLON suddenly realizes that the book he's pretending to read is turned upside down. He instantly turns it over the other way round.

VILLON: It is the ecclesiology you suggested I should work on, my Father, to train my memory. And I am learning *le Doctrinal* as well.

FATHER GUILLAUME smiles lovingly, gives him a slight clip on the back of the head, and sits down on the firm bed.

FATHER GUILLAUME: Oh, you fox! (*Laughs*) You thought you could trick the old man? Have you been out all night again, with your unreliable *friends* as you tend to call them?

VILLON: They *are* my friends, Father! (*Confused*) Well . . . yes, I was out . . .

FATHER GUILLAUME: What have you done this time? I hope that you've left Madame de Bruyeres alone! She still quivers nights after your prank with that stone monument—

VILLON, *his face brightens*: Le Pet-au-Diable! You should have seen the look on her face when we . . .

VILLON stops short and lowers his eyes, noticing the disapproving look on FATHER GUILLAUME's face.

FATHER GUILLAUME: I am relieved to see that you understand that such behavior is inappropriate, Francois. Your mother brought you here when you were a child. How old were you . . . twelve? You were such an innocent, angel-faced boy! She brought you here so that you become a learned, erudite, and bright man. And I am very upset to see that you are turning into a street ruffian instead! There is a great number of ruffians in the streets of weary, old Paris city! I don't want you to become one of them!

VILLON: I am very sorry to disappoint you, Father!

VILLON stands up from the chair and lays his hand on his heart.

VILLON: And here is my vow to you: I, Franciscus de Montcorbier, from now on known as Francois Villon, will turn over a new leaf, I will reform.

VILLON comes up to FATHER GUILLAUME. He kneels before the priest and puts his head on FATHER GUILLAUME's lap.
    FATHER GUILLAUME softens and strokes VILLON on his head.

FATHER GUILLAUME: Martha has heated a bowl of water, you can go take a bath and wash the smell of dusty streets off.

VILLON kisses FATHER GUILLAUME's hand and stands up on his feet, ready to leave the room, but FATHER GUILLAUME stops him.

FATHER GUILLAUME: Francois! I need to have a talk with you about . . . I fret myself about the kind of acquaintances you strike up. It well may be that Regnier de Montigny descends from a noble family, but he has an extremely bad influence on you! And a certain Colin de Cayeulx, your new friend . . . that bandit whose bones will be hanging at Montfaucon one day—

VILLON: Father! He is an educated and *deep* man.

FATHER GUILLAUME: As deep as a beer tun! My son, you would never have become a habitué of taverns if it were not for these demons that pulled you there!

VILLON: The Sorbonne itself drove me to the road leading to the taverns! Sorbonne's show-offs and its crazy jargon! Oh, how harsh and disgusting that language sounded to me at first! And maybe that kind of language is inappropriate, but at least the knowledge of it proves useful to me! It is highly approved in taverns!

VILLON sits under the writing table like an offended child.

FATHER GUILLAUME: Francois, think of your mother! The poor woman will lose her mind if she realizes that her only son is willing to burn in the flames of Hell for his sins! Francois, take pity on you! You can become a priest. I will help you. I have brought you up, taught you how to read and write! I have been paying all of your college expenses for all these years!

VILLON jumps to his feet resolutely and starts pacing the room back and forth.

VILLON: I will take my Licentiate and my degree of Master of Arts! I will not fail you or your expectations of me, Father! But remember your priceless days of youth! Those days have gone, never to return. "Those are the snows of yester-year" that we will never be able to bring back. Early in life we all have this restless fire inside, and we desperately want to submit to it. Isn't it true, Father? And what if I do succumb to it! These days will be gone at that very instant. But I will have my memories, memories of the fun I used to have. Maybe it will even help me understand different people and their lives better! Isn't that what Averroes teaches us? "Observe, understand and learn!" (*He sighs.*) Anyway, we all have to live with our sins—

FATHER GUILLAUME: My dear boy, you don't have to! Our merciful God forgives those who repent their sins!

VILLON sits on the bed near FATHER GUILLAUME.
    They are silent for a while.

FATHER GUILLAUME: Well, as long as you promise me to change your way of life and focus irrevocably on your studies! You know, sometimes I wish I were more strict and abrupt with you. Not as much as our teachers of course. They violate our conventional rules and moral principles by beating students. (*Crosses himself.*) But maybe just a little more strict to call you to order.

VILLON buries his face in the priest's shoulder.

FATHER GUILLAUME, *anxious*: Francois, tell me, is the money I give you not enough to buy some food? You have become very emaciated and pale lately.

VILLON: Father, "Qui m'a este plus doux que mere," the goodness of your heart knows no bounds—

FATHER GUILLAUME: Francois, what do you spend your money on?

VILLON: On pleasure . . . of being satisfied and full and cheerful.

FATHER GUILLAUME nods his head.

FATHER GUILLAUME: You surely know how to manipulate the words, my boy, and you know different shades of their meanings. I believe that you behave reasonably and know that a wise man once said that money can't buy everything . . . But enough of this. I have bored you enough with my dogmata for today! Here, take that . . .

FATHER GUILLAUME shakes two golden ecu out from a small red cloth bag and offers them to VILLON.

VILLON: I thank you, Father!

VILLON kisses FATHER GUILLAUME's hand, takes the money, and playfully tosses the coins up on his palm.
   FATHER GUILLAUME heads for the door.

The sounds of a bustle can be heard coming from the street. Somebody starts throwing pebbles into the fling-open window shutter.
   VILLON moves backward to the window.
   FATHER GUILLAUME stops and turns around.

FATHER GUILLAUME: I brought you a gift, Francois. A book—the most precious of all gifts.

FATHER GUILLAUME pulls a thick book in a green hardcover leather from under his frock.
   VILLON comes closer and takes the book in his hands.

VILLON: *Le Roman de la Rose.*

VILLON runs his fingers over the book's binding and cover.

FATHER GUILLAUME: I know how much you wanted to read this book. I sincerely hope that this reading will distract you from your nighttime outings!

VILLON: I don't know how to thank you for that, my Father!

FATHER GUILLAUME smiles and exits.

Someone continues throwing pebbles into the window shutter.
   One of the pebbles hits VILLON in the back of his head.

VILLON: Ow!

VILLON rubs the back of his head and leans out of the window.

Below, among the bushes, stands REGNIER DE MONTIGNY, VILLON's friend since childhood.

MONTIGNY whistles.

He is dressed in good taste as usual. His clothing is expensive but frayed, and he is wearing a provocative huge wide-brimmed hat.

VILLON puts the book on the table, puts the coins away into the little bag attached to his waistband, and hastily climbs out of the window.

As soon as VILLON appears beside him . . .

MONTIGNY : Apparently, Guillaume de Villon decided to lecture you . . .

VILLON: He gave me *Le Roman de la Rose*!

MONTIGNY: That's generous! Bring it with you tomorrow, I'd love to leaf that book through! But enough of this! Are you ready for an adventure?

VILLON, *smiling playfully*: As I always am. Always ready for the most fascinating and dangerous adventure named life!

MONTIGNY and VILLON leave the garden through the garden gate and appear on the crowded street Rue de Fuarre.

VILLON: I have to spend this night in my bed, if you know what I mean. I owe it to Father, Regnier.

MONTIGNY: Don't worry! You will! Tonight Colin and I have some business to do. *Personal* business, and you are not the part of our company for tonight.

VILLON, *intrigued*: What kind of business?

MONTIGNY: You'll know when the time is right.

VILLON: It's not fair! At first you speak a very strange and incomprehensible language, and now you don't even let me into your conspiracy or "business"!

MONTIGNY: You'll know when the time is right. Hurry up now! Colin is already waiting for us at the Mule tavern!

VILLON, *cheers up*: It's tremendous when you can escape with relief from those frigid, angular classrooms you see every day, from Averroes, Aristotle, logic that leads nowhere, metaphysics, and black-robed metaphysicians to the warm shelter of a tavern, a good glass of wine, and the company of human beings!

MONTIGNY smiles complacently.
    VILLON and MONTIGNY exit in a hurry.

Blackout.

Scene 3

My clerks, like bird-lime gripping all,
When out upon the prigging lay
Or robbing, watch your skins I pray:
For following these pastimes twain
Colin de Cayeulx had to pay.

The tavern Mule.

It's hot and stifling inside.

The revelry is in full swing.

The multifarious folk, both drunk and sober, drink wine and belt out songs.

A group of university scholars sitting at the round table are in the midst of a heated discussion. One of the scholars occasionally smashes his fist down on the table and blurts out some quotations from Aristotle.

Enter VILLON and MONTIGNY.

They chuckle and look round the tavern.

MONTIGNY nudges VILLON.

MONTIGNY: Ah! There he is!

MONTIGNY elbows his way toward the wooden table, hidden in the far niche.

VILLON follows.

They approach the table where sits COLIN DE CAYEULX, the son of a locksmith of the quarter, a hardened blackguard.

COLIN: At last! Where the devil have you been?

MONTIGNY and VILLON sit down.

MONTIGNY, *grins*: Guillaume has been issuing reprimands to our little boy Francois!

VILLON, *vexed and irritated*: Regnier, stop mocking me! This is no fun at all!

MONTIGNY, *shouts*: GUILLEMETTE! SERVE UP AND BRING US WINE!

A flushing red-haired girl jumps up from one of the scholars' knees and rushes toward the little far door leading to the wine cellar.

COLIN, *to MONTIGNY*: So did you get the money?

VILLON: Money? What for?

MONTIGNY: Well, aren't you a little gawker!

COLIN disregards VILLON's interference.

COLIN, *to MONTIGNY*: Listen to me, Regnier! The Coquillards won't wait longer! They want to get our fee tonight before the dawn.

VILLON: Who are those Coquillards? What are you talking about?

MONTIGNY: Let alone! I told you, you will find out when the time is right.

VILLON: The time is never right for you to tell me about your "secret" business! You know what? I am leaving! I am leaving right now!

VILLON remains seated.

COLIN: Wait, little one. Have you got your easy money on you?

VILLON, *cheers up*: Yes, I do. And I am eager to offer it for the good of *our* cause!

COLIN: I think we can test him, what do you think?

MONTIGNY: Well . . . if our little Francois is all grown up . . .

VILLON, *passionately*: Yes, I am, and I am ready! I will do anything!

MONTIGNY: Be more careful with the words you say. You never know when the devil can overhear you!

MONTIGNY smiles insidiously.

COLIN: Then don't waste your time! See that pork leg? Guillemette has just served it for that fatso. Go save him from the gluttony and steal the leg!

VILLON looks at COLIN, bewildered. But without giving it a second thought, goes to the fatso, who is just about to swallow the whole pork leg at once.
    VILLON pats the fatso on his shoulder and joins him at the table. They talk and laugh unconstrainedly for a while.

COLIN: Hm, not bad! But let's assist our newly fledged sneak thief!

COLIN drops an iron dish that was standing on the table to the floor. It crashes onto the floor loudly.
    VILLON jumps to his feet and pretends to be startled. He topples over his chair.

VILLON, *shouts*: THE SERGEANTS! THEY ARE HERE!

Everyone starts looking around, whispering to one another. Those who are not absolutely drunk and can still stand on their feet run to the windows and lean out to see where the guards are.
    The fatso slips his shabby cloak over his shoulders and exits the tavern in a hurry.

Meanwhile, VILLON snatches the pork leg from the dish and makes his way toward his table, where his friends are choking with laughter.
    The idlers return to their tables, and the merriment continues.

MONTIGNY and COLIN laugh.

COLIN, *lifts his tankard*: I praise thee, Francois de Villon! You have officially become one of us! That is your second christening. Remember this day! Yet I have so much to teach you! How to steal fish—

MONTIGNY: How to steal wine . . . I love your wine-turning-into-water trick!

COLIN: And how to steal many other useful and pleasant things from the naive people!

MONTIGNY: Let us drink to the inevitable temptations of life that lie round each and every corner in wait for us, and let our mischief go unpunished!

VILLON, MONTIGNY, and COLIN laugh loudly, raise and clink their tankards.
    At this very moment, a drunken CLERK approaches their table in an unstable waddle.

CLERK: I greet thee, oh daredevils of Sorbonne! (*He belches.*)

The CLERK falls under the table.
    VILLON and MONTIGNY look under the table and roar with laughter.

VILLON: Only in Paris one can have such a prolonged encounter with a drunk clerk!

COLIN: You, drunk swine! (*He gives the clerk a push with his foot.*) Regnier, help me scratch that scoundrel off the floor!

While COLIN and MONTIGNY help the CLERK to stand up and seat him on the bench, he sobs.

COLIN: There! Now, you drunken bum, are you weak in the head?

CLERK: I can prove you're wrong. Listen . . . (*He lifts his index finger.*) "So nimble, and so full of s-s-subtle flame, As if-f-f that every one from when-n-n-ce . . . they came . . ." Em-m-m . . . No, wait! Now! I remember . . . "Had meant to put his whole wit in a j-je-s-s-st."

MONTIGNY: He still manages to quote *Metamorphoses*! That means he is not *hopelessly* drunk!

The CLERK hangs his head and starts mumbling an indecent tavern song.

MONTIGNY, *to CLERK*: Listen, my good man, would you care to join us in our Marelle board game? We need another player after all!

VILLON: What the hell are you talking about, Regnier? We are not playing—

MONTIGNY: But of course we are! (*Rudely draws VILLON closer and whispers in his ear.*) Francois, don't make me blow this chance! You are out of your mind! The game is so rich with opportunities of trickery! He will lose all the money he has!

COLIN: Francois, my boy, why don't you go find Jeanette and have some fun with her! I just saw her heading for her room . . . (*He gives VILLON a dirty smirk.*) Go! But for the sake of all the wine tuns of the Paris City, don't bark at the moon reciting poetry! She is *not* fond of romance.

VILLON frowns, sighs, and retires unwillingly. He goes toward the little far door in the left part of the tavern and disappears behind it.

Meanwhile, MONTIGNY and the CLERK start playing the Marelle game. MONTIGNY lays out little numbered pebbles on the table and begins to cover the ones lying on the CLERK's part of the table with his own little gray stones and counts the numbers.
    COLIN joins the merriment of the university scholars, who sit at the round table.
    The loud tavern music drowns the sounds of voices in the tavern.
    MONTIGNY suddenly jumps to his feet, looking infuriated. He snatches his iron tankard and throws it with all might into the CLERK's head.
    Nobody takes notice of that. The CLERK screams.
    But at the same time, a red-haired scholar knocks down a burly man. And the fight begins.
    The music comes abruptly to an end, the majority of tavern callers gather round the fighting men and whistle, cheer loudly, and dispute about who will win.

COLIN goes to MONTIGNY's table. MONTIGNY stands near the CLERK, who sprawls on the bench. MONTIGNY is shaking and panting. He grips a dagger in his hand.
    COLIN pushes MONTIGNY toward the tavern exit. MONTIGNY runs as fast as his legs will carry him out of the tavern.
    VILLON peeps out through the door. COLIN grabs his hand and shoves the completely uncomprehending VILLON out of the tavern.

VILLON: What happened? Where is Montigny?

As they pass the table where the CLERK is seated, VILLON steps into blood that trickles down to the floor under the bench.

VILLON: There is blood! Blood! He is dead!

COLIN: As we all will be one day! Stop screaming, we don't need to attract attention! Go!

COLIN pushes VILLON to the exit. VILLON turns round in horror.
    They leave the tavern.
    The women's howls and screams can be heard from the tavern.

Blackout.

Scene 4

The Marriage of the Sow and the Bear

Two days later.

Late evening.

VILLON and MONTIGNY sit on a low stone fence around the little garden adjoining the Royal Precinct.

VILLON sits on the fence and wiggles his foot lightheartedly.

MONTIGNY peers at the dark alley opposite the garden.

VILLON: Your luck is good, Regnier! Two days have passed, and the guards are still not on your track! Nobody suspects or even remembers you being in the Mule that night.

MONTIGNY gives him a complacent smile.

MONTIGNY: Oh sure enough! Fortune smiles on me occasionally! However, I really wonder if there will be a catch in it waiting for me somewhere round the corner one day . . . But you know what, Francois? That was a lively night back then! All of my organs and senses were aroused especially when I had cut the little bag full of money off the dead clerk's waistband.

VILLON: So what are you going to do with the money?

MONTIGNY: Colin has it. We still need to pay the admission fee that the Coquillards are waiting for. You've heard of that, I suppose? But don't even start questioning who these people are, where, why, and blah-blah-blah . . .

VILLON looks at MONTIGNY and sighs, annoyed.

VILLON and MONTIGNY: You'll know when the time is right!

VILLON, *irritated*: Right! I have learned that lesson already! So . . . it's just you and me tonight?

MONTIGNY nods.

VILLON: Are we going to visit the tavern of Grosse Margot?

MONTIGNY: No, my naive mate! We have a new turn for your fast filly! You remember how our *Pet-au-Diable* stone has been stolen from us recently? But you did a great job, assembling our Sorbonne pals and returning the stone to our special place on Mont Saint-Hilaire. The scholars were heartened by your enthusiasm, they followed you as their leader! But there's a thought that haunts me: Why drag the Sow along all the time? I believe it's lonely!

VILLON looks excited.
    MONTIGNY gives him a long piercing look.
    VILLON grows impatient.

VILLON: Well, say it already!

MONTIGNY: I believe, our Sow needs a spouse! And I know where to find an adequate match for her!

VILLON, *considerably cheered up*: Where on earth? Do I know this place?

MONTIGNY: Right there!

MONTIGNY points in the direction of the Royal Precinct.

Loud steps can be heard coming from the dark alley opposite the garden. The group of SCHOLARS appears carrying the torches. They approach VILLON and MONTIGNY.
    MONTIGNY and VILLON smile to them, and they all exchange glances silently.
    GUY TABARIE comes forward. They whisper something to one another with VILLON.

VILLON, *in a constrained voice*: My dear friends, are we ready to save our Sow from loneliness? Are we ready to besiege this royal fortress and steal the Bear?

MONTIGNY: Our new target is the big long stone, and from now on, we shall name him—the Bear!

SCHOLARS cheer approvingly.
VILLON takes one of the torches from a SCHOLAR and lifts it overhead.

VILLON: Follow me and let's *kill* the loneliness and *save the Sow!*

The SCHOLARS follow VILLON toward the Royal Precinct's wooden gates.
They have their torches overhead, and they cheer half-whispering, "KILL! KILL! SAVE THE SOW! KILL! KILL! SAVE THE SOW!"
On their way, they steal butcher's hooks and ropes from the nearest stores.
When the group approaches the gates, VILLON stops, turns round, and faces the crowd.

VILLON: Now! We divide into groups! Group one—six scholars, stay here and break the gates open! Group two—others, come with me into the precinct!

SCHOLARS start wrenching the wooden gates with their hooks. VILLON, accompanied by MONTIGNY and other SCHOLARS, climbs over the stone fence.
VILLON's voice can be heard from behind the fence.

VILLON: DONE, MATES! HURRY UP WITH THE GATES OVER THERE!

The SCHOLARS finally fling the gates open. Meanwhile, the rest of the gang is already knocking down the big long stone. The newcomers bring the old wooden cart, and they all load the heavy stone on the cart and drag it out of the gates.
The procession, lead by VILLON and MONTIGNY, reaches the middle of the street, and VILLON signals at them to stop.

VILLON: We are about to marry our Sow with the Bear! But what is the marriage without guests or priests?

SCHOLARS cheer loudly. One of the SCHOLARS standing closer to MONTIGNY screams.

SCHOLAR: THE TAVERN SIGNS WILL BE OUR WEDDING GUESTS!

VILLON: THE CEREMONY WILL BE PERFORMED BY THE *STAG* SIGN! WITH THE *POPINJAY* ASSISTING! GO EVERYONE AND INVITE OUR GUESTS!

MONTIGNY: OUR COUPLE WILL BE KNOWN AS THE SOW AND THE BEAR!

The SCHOLARS run along the street and tear the tavern signs down. They steal colorful fabrics, smashing the windows of the stores.
VILLON and MONTIGNY, with the help of GUY TABARIE, who pushes the cart from behind, drag the stone forward.
The SCHOLARS hollo loudly and frisk about the cart like imps.

The windows of the houses surrounding the street start to open, and the horrified faces of the drowsy townsfolk stare at the noisy procession.

GUY TABARIE climbs up the stone and puts a hat on it.

VILLON, *to MONTIGNY*: Sunday will become our feast day, and we'll dance around our Bear on the Mount Genevieve every night to the sound of flutes and drums!

MONTIGNY: And we'll force all passersby and especially the king's officers to swear to preserve the privileges of the Bear!

GUY TABARIE: We will fix it by means of thick bands of iron and plaster, and no one will be able to steal it from us again! *Ever!*

VILLON, MONTIGNY, and GUY TABARIE pinpoint out of sight in the dark alley.

Suddenly, the whistles of the GUARDS can be heard in the distance.
SCHOLARS run toward the dark alley.

SCHOLAR: Hurry up! (*Trying to catch his breath.*) Hurry up, mates! Remi has already been kicked to death, he fell off the ladder, and the guards finished him off! Every man for himseeelf!

The SCHOLARS speed away in a bustling crowd.

Blackout.

PART 2

Scene 1

Harsh justice his behind did flay
And make him seek in exile flight;
In vain' twas: "I appeal" to say,
A law term not too recondite.
Eternal rest be his for aye.

The Priest Chermoye

Cool summer evening of June 5, 1455.

The Feast of Corpus Christi.

The Sacred Procession of the Body of God has just finished.

The streets are still overloaded with the rose petals, especially the street of Saint-Jacques that lies right in front of the Saint-Benoit Church.

People close their wide-open windows and remove the rich cloths and tapestries that hang from the windows.

The street is mostly illuminated by the temporary altars that stand along the street of Saint-Jacques, decked with flowers, silks, and lighted tapers.

VILLON sits on the steps of the Saint-Benoit chapel. He slips the light black cloak on and dips his feet into the rose petals.

GILLES, the priest, and ISABEL, the beautiful lady that lives in the neighborhood, sit next to VILLON.

VILLON sniffs the cool air approvingly.

VILLON: Oh, how wonderful! This evening is truly a blessed one! After all the heat and dust of the day, it feels so reviving. Just smell this pure air!

VILLON smiles and gives a deep sigh.
ISABEL slightly touches his hand.

ISABEL: Don't you also sense that intoxicating aroma of the cherry trees?

ISABEL smiles flirtatiously.
VILLON laughs and kisses her cheek.

GILLES: And I can still smell those delicious fatted fowls and capons . . . Hmmmm! The supper at the House of the Red Door is second to none as usual!

ISABEL: I admire this feast every year! The city rejoices at it.

The many-colored procession of Corpus Christi passes through the streets, the children strew the flowers around, the white-robed singing men raise a loud song, servers bear lighted candles and flaming wax torches, the thurifers with silver censers toss clouds of white fragrant smoke into the summer air, more lights, more singers, [*Getting more and more excited.*] more friars and monks and beadles appear in the streets, and the populace joins and follows the Sacred Host in its precious monstrance born by the celebrating priests under a canopy rich with cloth of gold and tassels, the bells ring and the chanting—

GILLES: I want to thank you, Francois, and Father Guillaume for inviting us to join you for supper! As for me, I don't *admire* the heavy smell of flowers and incense and hot wax and the dust stirred up by so many slow-moving feet . . . (*He grins at Isabel.*) But the supper and such a conciliative pastime brought me joy tonight, I thank you!

VILLON: And you are very welcome! I, on my behalf, apologize for not keeping up the conversation this evening. It is a special day for every believer, and my mind is just full of different thoughts and questions, and my heart is pounding in time with the sacred chantings.

GILLES: For that I praise thee, Master Francois!

PHILIPPE CHERMOYE, the drunk priest, and his drinking companion, Master JEHAN LE MARDI, approach the chapel.

CHERMOYE swears maliciously and spits.
CHERMOYE notices VILLON and screams.

CHERMOYE: By God! I have found you! Maitre Francois, there you are! I swear by the Lord, you won't be the better off! I will heat your ears for you!

VILLON rises to make room for the drunk priest.

VILLON: Sweet sir, what angers you? Monsignor, why are you being angry with me? Have I wronged you? What do you want with me? I do not think I have ever harmed you. So what is my guilt?

CHERMOYE gets infuriated and pushes VILLON backward so strongly that he is forced to sit down again.
    VILLON becomes inflamed.

VILLON: Are you looking for a chance to start a fight, Monsignor?

CHERMOYE laughs coarsely and spits.
    The tower clock strikes nine.

GILLES, to CHERMOYE and LE MARDI: Dear Sirs, I suggest you leave us severely alone! It would be better if you retire!

LE MARDI: Oh, we didn't suppose this street belongs to you and we are so unwanted here!

GILLES rises and approaches LE MARDI.

GILLES: Monsignor, you both are drunk! I suggest you leave! It is a terrible sin to get drunk on such a special sacred day! Go and pray for forgiveness of your sins!

VILLON is spoiling for a fight. ISABEL clutches at his shoulder and tries to calm him down.

CHERMOYE: YSABEAU! Isn't that your name? Oh, what a delicious peach!

VILLON: How dare you!

ISABEL: Francois, Francois, dear, don't!

CHERMOYE: Yes, *Francois, dear* . . . having a good time with another harlot? (*He hiccups.*) Which tavern does she come from? I would like to meet her friends there . . . if the other whores are as pretty as she is! (*He starts making vulgar movements as if he's making love to her.*)

ISABEL: Oh my honor!

VILLON: YOU RASCAL!

VILLON throws himself at CHERMOYE. The drunk priest draws a large dagger from beneath his gown and strikes VILLON in the face with it. He cuts VILLON's upper lip, causing thereby a great flow of blood.

    ISABEL screams and starts to cry. GILLES comes running up to ISABEL and tries to lead her away from the place where the real bloody fight unfolds itself.

ISABEL: FRANCOIS! NO! HE IS DRUNK! HE IS MAD! RUN! FRANCOIS!

GILLES: Isabel, my dear girl! Francois knows what he is doing! He'll escape! But now, he would want you to leave this place! I'll take you to my church, you'll be safe there!

ISABEL, *trying to break free*: I won't leave him! Chermoye will kill him! FRANCOIS!

GILLES leads ISABEL away.

Meanwhile, VILLON draws a dagger from beneath his cloak and strikes the infuriated priest in the groin or thereabouts. CHERMOYE screams, but he is carried away by fury, so he pursues VILLON, who is trying to withdraw, hurls several threats, and menaces. He tries to hit Francois harder.

    Suddenly, LE MARDI, who had vanished into thin air when the fight began, reappears behind CHERMOYE.

    LE MARDI tries to disarm VILLON, but VILLON entices CHERMOYE and LE MARDI into the courtyard of Saint Benedict's Church. There he picks up a stone from the ground, and when CHERMOYE tries to attack him again, he throws the stone into CHERMOYE's face. The priest falls onto the pavement.

VILLON takes to his heels.

VILLON turns round, running. The people gather round CHERMOYE.
  LE MARDI is cut off by the crowd.
  The voices can be heard from behind.

MAN 1: We need to dress his wounds!

WOMAN 1: Take the dagger away from him!

MAN 2: Oh my! He clings to it!

WOMAN 2: Carry him to the nearest house!

MAN 2: Ready? Lift him up! Let's carry him into the prison house of the Saint-Benoit!

VILLON hurries away to the nearest shop of a barber-surgeon.

Blackout.

Scene 2

They cannot blame me justly here,
Except that others paid too dear.
I tell the truth and nothing less,
And speak this boast with conscience clear;
Who did no wrong need not confess

Half an hour later.

The gloomy side street adjoining the street of Saint-Jacques.

The sound of careless voices talking together and now and then a stave of raucous song can be heard coming from the Mule tavern in the neighboring street.

The air is still and clear.

VILLON hastily approaches the shop of the barber-surgeon, FOUQUET. He gazes round and knocks.

FOUQUET shouts from behind the door.

FOUQUET: Since the devil's brought you here, come in!

VILLON enters the lopsided, old house.

The warm, unsteady light coming from the fireplace illuminates the room, blocked up with chairs, bales, and other lumber.

Fat FOUQUET notices VILLON's bleeding lip.

FOUQUET: Oh, merciful God! Sit down, monsieur, sit down! I will attend to your wound immediately!

VILLON: I don't know how to thank you, Fouquet!

FOUQUET examines VILLON's lip. He pants.

FOUQUET, *smiling*: Well, what did you fight for?

FOUQUET goes to an old chest and starts to fumble in it. He returns holding a needle and a red-hot iron plate.

FOUQUET: I need to cauterize the wound, it will hurt! Wait! I have a duty to perform, you know. For the purpose of making my report to the watch, I need to know the names of the parties in the quarrel.

VILLON sighs.

VILLON: Oh, the severe accursed regulations of the watch. My assailant was a priest named Philippe Chermoye.

VILLON stops short in confusion and looks at the needle in FOUQUET's hands. He gulps down a lump in his throat.

FOUQUET: And may I demand who you are?

VILLON: My name is Michel Mouton.

FOUQUET: All right, Monsieur Mouton, let us proceed! Try not to scream. I am growing deaf in here ... All the screaming ... (*Mutters*) I detest this quarter of colleges, fights, and empty money pouches!

FOUQUET bends over VILLON's wound and wheezes loudly.
    VILLON screws up his eyes, and as FOUQUET cauterizes the wound, VILLON quietly moans.

Blackout.

VILLON slips discreetly out of the shop.
    He slinks along the dark side street. Suddenly, he hears the rustling sound of somebody's cloak and wary footsteps behind his back.
    He hastens his pace. VILLON understands that he is being followed.
    VILLON presses himself against the wall in a feeble attempt to be concealed from the view of the persecutor under the cover of night.

The sound of the footsteps ceases.

VILLON takes a deep breath and moves away from the wall. He steps into the light.

VILLON examines the deserted street.

A motionless figure of a MAN wrapped in a dark cloak stands unnoticed behind him.

Suddenly, the MAN puts his hand on VILLON's shoulder.

VILLON instantly turns round, gasping.

The MAN chuckles softly and throws down the hood.

VILLON: Goddamn you, Regnier! Why the hell are you here?

MONTIGNY: I saw Isabel sobbing and running away from the House of the Red Door. I guessed that if there was unrest on the streets of old Paris City, you couldn't be not involved in it! I followed you up to Fouquet.

VILLON: Do you know about the fight?

MONTIGNY: Everything in detail! Paris is not good at keeping such events a secret.

VILLON: Is Chermoye . . . dead?

MONTIGNY: No, the old swine is still breathing. Francois, you are in grave danger! He will inform the watch against you! You must take to flight—

VILLON: I must escape! The cloister of Saint-Benoit, where I have seen Chermoye stagger and fall, is now closed to me. You must know . . . Tell it to Father Guillaume. Chermoye was the aggressor! He wanted to accomplish his wicked and damnable will! He . . . I found myself in a state of legitimate defense! It was self-defense! I was forced—

MONTIGNY: Stop jabbering! You have no single sympathetic witness to support this defense. Go to Porte Saint-Jacques! LISTEN TO ME!

VILLON lets out a sob.

MONTIGNY: There is a village of Bourg-la-Reine, on the Orleans road. About two leagues outside the walls of Paris. Go there. Find Perrot Girart, the barber. Perrot Girart!

VILLON: Perrot Girart, the barber—

MONTIGNY: He will give refuge to you. Keep a low profile for a couple of days.

VILLON: Regnier, in three days, before the bells of Paris will begin ringing Prime, I will be well beyond the walls and in the open country, making for the South!

MONTIGNY: You don't have three days, you dimwit! You have one night to escape!

VILLON: I have to explain everything to Isabel and Father Guillaume—

MONTIGNY: I will tell them all they need to know. Most importantly, you must flight Paris! Master Guillaume will intercede for the letter of remission. His honorable reputation and intimate acquaintances among the nobles of the law and of the Parliament are sure to facilitate the process of granting your clemency. Now! *You* have to get out of reach of justice, Francois!

VILLON: I am a . . . manslayer now, Regnier?

VILLON trembles with fear.

MONTIGNY: Not yet. The priest is still alive. And if he sobers up before his death, he has to repent his sins and forgive you as a respectable believer! We shall all pray for your forgiveness, little one.

MONTIGNY and VILLON approach the Porte Saint-Jacques.

MONTIGNY: Be careful if you don't want to come to the gallows! You are a bachelor of criminal arts, and you passed honorably in elementary bloodshed and advanced burglary. That enables me not to worry. You will not die of hunger.

MONTIGNY smiles warmly at VILLON.

VILLON: I am capable of snapping up an occasional duck or hen or grabbing a turnip from the field. I know how one should swiftly take heels from vengeance of indignant farmers and barking dogs.

MONTIGNY: How can we find a way of doing somebody for a good meal? Whoever can do that will be a master. And you are a master of your own Villoneries. I am proud of you, Francois. I will see you later, in the village!

VILLON and MONTIGNY embrace.

VILLON: I am very grateful to you, Regnier! You taught me how to survive. I will be awaiting news from Paris.

MONTIGNY: Go now. Don't waste another minute.

VILLON turns round and heads for the nearest side street.

MONTIGNY stops in amazement.

MONTIGNY: Why do you go back into the city's web?

VILLON waves his hand at MONTIGNY.

VILLON: I have to see Laurens first. (*As if holding back tears.*) Want to bid farewell . . . to my poor little old mother.

VILLON exits.

Blackout.

Scene 3

This danger to escape, I trow,
The best plan is to run away.
Adieu! I'm off to Angers now.

The Escape

The little lopsided, shabby house in one of the downcast side streets of Paris that crosses the street of Saint Denis by the Saint Denis Abbey.

The house consists of just one room with low ceiling, remindful of a cave. A little wooden table and three chairs stand by the window. A bed stands along the wall as if undersetting it. The glowing, coming from the fireplace, illuminates the room.

An elderly woman, the MOTHER of Francois Villon, sits on a bench in front of the fireplace and turns up the live coals.

Enter VILLON.

VILLON hastily closes the door behind him, but the naughty wind blows out the candles on the table nevertheless.

His MOTHER turns round and stands up to meet him.

MOTHER throws up her hands.

MOTHER: Francois! Oh, my precious boy!

They embrace. MOTHER kisses VILLON on his forehead.

MOTHER: I haven't seen you for such a long time! You look so pale and thin. What happened to you, my boy?

VILLON sits down on the bench and warms his feet and hands by the fire.

VILLON: Mother, you worry too much. I am fine. It's just raining outside, and the wind is howling as if the wolves have arrived from the forests again.

VILLON pulls a package from under his cloak and gives it to his MOTHER.

VILLON: Here, take this. Father Guillaume ordered me to give you this fresh pâté. He will not take no for an answer. Please?

MOTHER: Oh, he is so generous! I feel uneasy accepting his gifts. But he always insists that I do!

MOTHER smiles. She pours VILLON a glass of water and unwraps the pâté, puts it into a bowl.

MOTHER: Our Savior blessed us with this man! He has done so much for us. I remember how after your father went to meet our Maker, I took your little hand in mine, and we went to the chapel of Saint-Benoit-le-Betourne. Maitre Guillaume became your spiritual leader.

VILLON: Yes, Mother. He is more than a father to me.

MOTHER: He taught you well. Thanks to him, you are a discreet and scientific man. Thanks to him, you've read so many books. I wish I could read! I believe there is a whole new world in those books, but unfortunately, it's too late for me to find myself in that world. (*Smiles*)

VILLON: Mother, I am grateful to Maitre Guillaume for everything. And I realize now I should have been more diligent in my studies. Oh, Mother!

> Had I but studied hard, in truth,
> When I was young, nor played the fool,
> But been a very virtuous youth,
> I'd have a house and lie in wool.
> But ah! I ran away from school,

> A way that naughty children take.
> The words are written; with the dule
> Indeed my heart is like to break.

I owe him everything, including my name. Your little boy, Franciscus de Montcorbier, became the famous poet of Paris streets, and in every tavern you can hear people sing my verses, the verses of Francois Villon.

MOTHER: I am so proud of you, my little bluebird of happiness!

MOTHER observes his face closely.

VILLON: Mother . . .

MOTHER: Francois, you look tired. And, oh, that scar! Here, sit next to me and tell me what has happened to you. I see incredible sorrow in your eyes.

VILLON sits down at the table. He moves the bowl with the pâté closer to him. Takes a chunk of bread and starts dipping it in the pâté. He gets irritated and puts the bread aside.

VILLON stares at the candlelight.

VILLON: Mother, we need to talk. I am sure you've heard of the incident that occurred between me and priest Chermoye.

MOTHER: Yes, he provoked you to start a fight with him. But as far as I know, he forgave you. However, that's him who needs to beg forgiveness before God!

VILLON: Mother, he died three days ago in l'Hotel Dieu from a wound that I had inflicted on him that night.

MOTHER, *in a trembling voice:* Oh, Lady of Heaven!

MOTHER covers her mouth with her hand and cries.
    VILLON takes her hand.

VILLON, *whispers:* Mother, I have to leave Paris . . . And I don't know when I can return. But Maitre Guillaume will take care of you, he promised . . . And I will be fine, I will let you know . . . send you a note with Regnier de Montigny as soon as I get to Angers!

MOTHER: I know . . . I know . . . you have to leave. It is not safe for you here. Let me find my knapsack, I have some money. I don't need it.

MOTHER stands up and walks toward the bed. VILLON succeeds after her and clasps her in his arms.
    MOTHER cries silently.

VILLON: I don't need money. I am a seller of engravings now. I will earn money on my way. I want just to be with you now, look at you, hold your hand in mine. And I need to complete my work before I leave.

VILLON seats his MOTHER on the bed and sits down to the table. He gets yellowish sheets of paper, lights the candle, and puts it on the table in front of him.

VILLON: I am writing a Testament, which promises to be quite a fun! (*Laughs, with a heavy heart.*) I want you to give it to . . . No!

MOTHER lies down.

VILLON: I will start with a ballad. (*Starts writing.*) "Ballad that Villon made at the request of his mother, wherewithal to do her homage to our Lady . . ."

MOTHER: I will clasp this ballad to my heart and never let go of it! My heart is bleeding because you have to leave.

VILLON: Mother, I love you very much, and you know it! But it's for the better.

MOTHER: Francois, we'll all have to leave one day . . . in one way or another.

VILLON: But I will come back. Very soon.

MOTHER: I know. And I will be always waiting for your return and keeping the fireplace burning. I love you, my precious boy! My Francois Villon!

VILLON: Mother, you go to sleep, and while you are slumbering, I will be reading the ballad aloud for you.

MOTHER: You can start now. I would love to hear your ballad.

VILLON: It is your ballad, Mother. See? (*He starts writing.*)

>   Lady of Heaven, Regent of the earth,
>   Empress of all the infernal marshes fell,
>   Receive me, Thy poor Christian, 'spite my dearth,
>   In the fair midst of Thine elect to dwell.

VILLON turns round and sees that his MOTHER is already fast asleep.

VILLON: A poor old wife I am, and little worth:

>   Nothing I know, nor letter aye could spell:
>   Where in the church to worship I fare forth,
>   I see Heaven limned, with harps and luters, and Hell,
>   Where damned folk seethe in fire unquenchable . . .
>   Thou didst conceive, Princess most bright of sheen,
>   Jesus the Lord, that hath nor end nor mean,
>   Almighty, that, departing Heaven's demesne
>   To succour us, put on our frailty,
>   Offering to death His sweet of youth and green:
>   Such as He is, our Lord He is, I ween!
>   In this belief I will to live and die.

VILLON blows out the candle.
    Conciliative darkness fills the room.

Blackout.

Scene 4

And had my life been still misspent,
For such a sinner's punishment
To burn to ashes were too good!
'Tis need drives men to devilment
And hunger wolves to leave the wood.

That same summer night.
  Darkness and stillness have finally descended on the town.

Illuminating his way with a flickering torchlight, FRANCOIS VILLON slips beyond the walls of the city unobserved.
  He is wrapped in a dark cloak and carries a pouch filled with some old clothes.
  He stops for a second and breathes in the nighttime air.

VILLON: I will see you again, my Paris! So here and now, I entrust my life to my feet!

VILLON sighs and strokes his stomach.

He approaches the ancient great gibbet Montfaucon.
  The place is cloaked in an ominous fog. The moans of creaking ropes can be heard.
  The bodies of the condemned hang there, rotting and spun like tops by the winds.
  VILLON shudders.
  Suddenly he notices a company of young gallants and their girls having a picnic. They are laughing and having a midnight frolic.

VILLON scents the meal from afar and decides to be of company.

He puts his pouch on the ground, extinguishes the torchlight. VILLON picks up a crooked stick from the ground.

He chuckles and breaks it down into two even pieces. He fixes the sticks up to his beret, so they look like horns.

He wraps himself into his cloak, hiding half of his face, and slowly approaches the merry company.

VILLON suddenly descends like a thunderbolt, disguised as a devil.

VILLON: A MORT! FOR DEATH! FOR DEATH! A MORT!

He flourishes a club and a hook that he stole from the butcher's shop on his way out of Paris.

The startled company disperses in a rout, helter-skelter. Girls shriek.

GIRL 1: DEVIL! DEVIL!

GIRL 2, GIRL 3: HE CAME AFTER US! RUN! RUN!

MAN 1: SAVE YOURSELVES!

MAN 2: SAVE YOUR SOULS!

MAN 1 dashes up, others dash down, thinking of nothing now but their God.

MAN1, MAN 2: ST. JOHN SAVE OUR SOULS!
GIRL 1, GIRL 2: SAVE OUR LIVES! MERCIFUL GOD, HELP US!

The company vanishes from the spot, leaving there the bread, the wine, and the meat.

VILLON laughs and throws off his disguise.

VILLON: Well, bon appétit, Maitre Francois!

VILLON sits down to the feast and finishes everything with considerable pleasure.

The bodies swing overhead in full moonlight.

VILLON raises his glass of wine and addresses the hanged.

VILLON: Now here, now there, as the wind shifts its stead,

We swing and creak and rattle overhead,

No thimble dinted like our bird-pecked face.
Brothers, have heed and shun the life we led:
The rather pray, God grant us of His grace!

Prince Jesus, over all empowered,
Let us not fall into the Place of Dread,
But all our reckoning with the Fiend efface.
Folk, mock us not that are forspent and dead;
The rather pray, God grant us of His grace!

Blackout.

PART 3

Scene 1

The Banquet after the Famous Contest at Blois

Early evening of late summer 1457.

The dining chamber in the Blois castle.

The elongated chamber is illuminated with big medieval torches attached to the walls and a huge fireplace. There are dozens of candles on the table.
    The chamber looks like a jewelry box, with its ruby-red walls decorated with golden monograms.

CHARLES D'ORLEANS, the Duke of Orleans, renowned poet, sits at the head of the table. He sips wine from a golden goblet.
    POETS sit around the table. The atmosphere is tense.

FRANCOIS VILLON is among them. He tries to relieve the tension that reigns in the chamber. So he tells jokes to the poet sitting next to him. The poet is out of spirits and lets by all the jokes, chuckles artificially.

CHARLES D'ORLEANS gives a sign with his hand for silence.
    He lifts his goblet.

CHARLES D'ORLEANS: Venerable poets! I ask for your attention! Tonight is one of those momentous evenings when we celebrate the finishing of another poetic contest at Blois. As you all know, there is nothing that I value more than art, the art of poetry! Each and every one of you is an eminent poet! But the contest is a battle, and only one man can gain a victory. Today, we raise our goblets to our new victor—Maitre Francois Villon! Whose rhyme is stronger than the strongest wine and brighter than the brightest star!

POETS, *in unison*: To Maitre Villon! Whose rhyme is stronger than the strongest wine and brighter than the brightest star!

Enter the SERVANT with the main dish of the evening, hot and spiced veal.

The POETS start exchanging remarks with one another.
    The chamber becomes more and more animated.

MAITRE JACOTIN, the poet, clears his throat to attract attention.

MAITRE JACOTIN: I guess, most of the esteemed poets here will agree with me if I say that Maitre Villon's rhyme is also very catchy, and ... how shall I put it? Coarse. Tell me, maitre, is that why you are called "the poet of the streets"?

VILLON: Life itself is coarse, Maitre Jacotin. The truth is coarse, but there is beauty in that truth as well as there is beauty in those streets you've mentioned.

MAITRE JACOTIN: I won't even argue against your statement. There is a great deal of truth in what you say. In addition, nobody knows the streets better than a person who lives on them and *feels* them!

CHARLES D'ORLEANS, *interrupts*: The best poets are closer to nature! There is nothing more beautiful, inspiring and giving hope than the stars twinkling in the night sky.

VILLON: At least you avoid tossing and turning on the softest feather beds that drag your fattened sides like a swamp.

MAITRE JACOTIN angrily cuts off a piece of veal and pours more wine into his goblet.

CHARLES D'ORLEANS laughs heartily at VILLON's remark.

CHARLES D'ORLEANS: Maitre Villon, you have quite an entertaining worldview! I should say, you are certainly a rare personality!

VILLON:

> "Most clement Prince, I'd have you be aware
> That I'm like all, and yet apart and rare;
> Much understand, yet wit and knowledge shun:
> To have my wage again is all my care;
> Well entertained, rebuffed of every one."

MAITRE JACOTIN, *sarcastically:* Bravo, maitre! But don't lower your merits! (*He grins.*) As far as we know, you have never been rebuffed by a woman! Or I better say, a libertine—

CHARLES D'ORLEANS, *sighs:* Oh, gentlemen! "But where are the snows of yester-year?"

CHARLES D'ORLEANS smiles at VILLON, which makes MAITRE JACOTIN choke over with wine.

CHARLES D'ORLEANS: One thought concerns me almost every morning when I look into my niece's eyes: Don't we give too much liberty to our ladies? I fear that one day women will rule the world, not only with their beauty but also with their wit!

All POETS concur with the duke.

VILLON: You needn't worry about that, Your Lordship, beauty fades away even faster than the wit. Day after day, the beauty is being wasted. And by the end of the day, you see that women are "all coins which wear thin of gold."

MAITRE JACOTIN: You know the value of the coins so well. Surely, your experience of the Navarre College robbery has taught you a good lesson. By the way, is the case still open?

VILLON: Not that I know. So long I am here in Blois. When I return to Paris, I will certainly let you know.

VILLON gets irritated.

CHARLES D'ORLEANS: You should have more wine, Maitre Villon.

VILLON: So that "even his fear of God would go . . . Happier he who says No!" No. Thank you, Your Lordship. My goblet is full.

POETS nod in approval and discuss the inexhaustible wit of VILLON.
     CHARLES D'ORLEANS orders a servant to bring a new jug of wine.

MAITRE JACOTIN: That distich sounds awfully familiar. I saw it scribbled on a shabby shutter of a den's window. (*He spits the words out.*) The banality and tastelessness of those phrases convinced me that that couplet was created by a narrow-minded, vulgar innkeeper! Never thought I'd be given such honor to share the meal with that very blotter, author of those words!

VILLON stands up from his seat, takes his goblet of wine, and splashes it out on MAITRE JACOTIN'S face.

All POETS jump up and help MAITRE JACOTIN to dry himself.

Meanwhile, CHARLES D'ORLEANS doesn't move. He sits solemnly at the head of the table and smiles at VILLON with a pleased smile.

VILLON turns to face the duke and bows before him. Then he heads for the door to exit.

MAITRE JACOTIN screams and curses.
     There is confusion and fuss in the chamber.

MAITRE JACOTIN: MAITRE VILLON, YOU ARE A MEAN SWINE!

VILLON turns toward him, pulls an impressive greasy veal leg, which he has stolen from the table minutes earlier, from under his cloak and throws it at MAITRE JACOTIN, aiming at his head.

VILLON exits.

Blackout.

Scene 2

———

Had she, whom I have served of yore
So loyally with all my heart . . .
Had she but told me at the start
Her wishes, (Ah my vain regret!)
'Twould not have needed wizard's art
To draw back scatheless from her net.

Early spring.
    Cold and rainy evening. The fierce wind is roaring outside the tavern.
    FRANCOIS VILLON sits at the table in the far end of the local tavern, hastily writing down some lines of a poem on an old yellowed scrap of paper.
    CHRISTOPHE TURGIS, the taverner, approaches VILLON and puts down a big tankard full of wine on the table in front of him.
    VILLON takes no notice of CHRISTOPHE and continues to write.

CHRISTOPHE: Still practicing your love ballads?

VILLON raises his head and looks at CHRISTOPHE.

VILLON: Still hoping that the pity will move her.

VILLON takes a sip and spits out the wine back into the tankard.
    He makes a wry face.

VILLON: Warm wine? The worst I've ever tasted!

CHRISTOPHE: Be content with what you are given. There was no place for the tun in our cellar. I had to keep it inside the tavern.

———

VILLON: So you give me wine from the tun that stands near the fireplace?

CHRISTOPHE: You give me more money, I'll bring you the wine from the cellar.

VILLON sighs.

VILLON: I have tried honest living, selling engravings, and failed. I have tried to love with pure and steadfast love and failed. You know, Christophe, honest liking is pretense, by rank falsehood truth is spread, and only lovers have sound sense.

VILLON grins bitterly.

VILLON: Now my heart and my purse (*he flings his near-empty purse onto the table*) are both wounded to death, Christophe.

CHRISTOPHE: I believe you make more sense when you are drunk. Listen, Francois, my boy, do you honestly think that this lady of the twisted nose, this coldhearted demoiselle of yours can love you? You! The queer, dark, dry, sharp-tongued scarecrow from Paris? Trust the old man, she may be attracted for a time to you, the moping poet, amused and flattered by your verses . . . but only for a time. She is using you, and soon Katherine will grow tired and throw you away.

VILLON: I am drunk with love. I cannot get her image out of my heart.

CHRISTOPHE: You are turning into a furnace of sighs, a melancholy Don of old comedies!

VILLON: I may as well be the lover flouted and cast off, but she does have a heart, and Katherine will respond to my love and passion. I know that. Don't contradict, old fool!

CHRISTOPHE: I may be old, but you are the one who is being led by the nose here. She is a bourgeois. It is rumored that she is married. You are a poor poet in hiding, having nothing more but shabby clothes, empty purse—

VILLON: My dear Rose! She leads me with dissimulation and sugared lies, fooling for her amusement and lets me open my heart to her, but only to make mock of me, she fooled me! Making me believe always one thing to be another!

CHRISTOPHE: Morning to be evening, small beer new wine, the clouds to be made of calfskin—

VILLON: Who made me swallow such humiliations but Katherine de Vaucelles?

VILLON gasps for air. He turns around to look at the flame raging in the fireplace.

CHRISTOPHE: I know one perfect remedy that will heal your wounds! Cold good wine of Arbois scented of raspberries.

CHRISTOPHE gets up and heads for the cellar, whistling happily on his way.

CHRISTOPHE, *humming:* Oh, faithless harlot de Vaucelles,
For love of money she will sell
Her body to a lustful pal!

CHRISTOPHE exits.

VILLON: Oh, faithless Katherine de Vaucelles!

VILLON turns back to the table and continues to write down his poem even more passionately than before.

Blackout.

Paris. Late at night.
　　The narrow street near the Saint-Benoit cloister.
　　VILLON cautiously makes his way along the wall of a luxurious house.

He notices the light in the window above him.
　　VILLON throws off his cloak and pulls out a folded sheet of yellowed paper.
　　He steps a little aside, faces the illuminated window, and clears his throat.

VILLON: "O, ma chiere rose!" Ma Katherine de Vaucelles!

> "As I believe, she showed me favour
> With soft regrets and fine deceit
> To lend duplicity more savour
> And make my overthrow complete."

The window swings open, and KATHERINE DE VAUCELLES looks out.

She is wearing a fur-edged gown, closely sheathing her slim body, heart-shaped velvet headdress.

Her hard dark eyes discern VILLON's figure in the dusk.

KATHERINE: What are you doing here, you feeble-minded man?

VILLON: I've put my love for you into a ballad, demoiselle.

> "Full harsh and hard was her oppression;
> For she who cast a spell on me—"

KATHERINE: Stop this noise!

VILLON, *even louder:*

> "Though I am guiltless of transgression,
> Has doomed me die, and her decree
> Is fixed that I shall cease to be."

The windows of the neighboring houses start to open; people lean out of the windows and express their outrage.

KATHERINE: GUARDS! GUARDS! THIS MAN HAS TO BE WHIPPED BY JUSTICE! GUARDS!

VILLON:

> "I find no safety but in flight.
> She means to break my life, I see,
> Nor will take pity on my plight."

GUARD: IN THE NAME OF THE KING OF FRANCE, DON'T MOVE!

The GUARDS surround VILLON. He realizes that he is trapped. But it's too late. There is no way out.

The GUARDS seize VILLON and start beating him.

VILLON falls to the ground.

The people shout cheers.

While the GUARDS fall on the troublemaker and even start beating each other without distinction, cursing, and screaming, VILLON manages to squeeze through the heap of GUARDS and escape the battlefield.

He stands for a minute catching his breath, looking at the scuffle.

In a second, VILLON takes to his heels and darts toward the gates Porte Saint-Jacques.

Blackout.

Scene 3

I laugh through tears, expect sans hope soe'er
And comfort take amiddleward despair;
Glad, though I joy in nought beneath the sun,
Potent am I, and yet as weak as air;
Well entertained, rebuffed of every one.

A small shabby lodging in an attic of a roadside tavern in the outskirts of Orleans.

Late summer morning. The sun is trying to emerge from behind the thick dark clouds.

VILLON sprawls on the old uncomfortable bed, half-naked.

BLANCHE, a young attractive wench, sits on the edge of the bed and pulls on her stockings.

VILLON stretches himself and sits up, yawning.

BLANCHE turns round and smiles. She notices a new dark-blue cloak, lying on the floor near the bed.

BLANCHE: Did it belong to a nobleman, your new cloak?

VILLON: As a matter of fact, it belonged to a wandering juggler. He stole it from a nobleman.

BLANCHE: And you stole it from him.

VILLON: Yes.

BLANCHE: Why did you come back? I didn't expect to see you again.

VILLON: I didn't want to lie idly through the endless night of June on my back in wheat fields, staring at the sky. I didn't want to be alone.

VILLON puts his arms around BLANCHE. She giggles.

BLANCHE, *flirting:* You know who you are?

VILLON: I know all save myself alone! I have wondered about half of France, lying at night now under a duke's roof and now in a filthy doss-house, now under a hedge, now in a wench's chamber, now in prison awaiting the morning's questioning, now again in a duke's house, and again in a wench's chamber. Every so often asking myself lying awake at night, who am I?

BLANCHE: Compared to the boozy clowns of this tavern, you are an honest man. And a sweet seducer . . .

BLANCHE bends forward to kiss him, but VILLON sharply turns away and stands up. He starts pacing the room back and forth angrily, putting on his shirt.

VILLON: An *honest man?* Are you out of your mind? I lied, I stole everything I could lay my fingers on, I robbed, I even committed sacrilege more than once, I whipped out my knife in a fight more than once—

BLANCHE: And who didn't? I have never met a man around here who didn't. How do you know? Maybe I stole too. Maybe I killed a person myself! From what I know, you at least pay me every time!

VILLON stands still by the window.
    BLANCHE approaches VILLON and puts her head on his shoulder. They both observe the first raindrops falling from the sky.

BLANCHE: My mother had a dream. Her daughter being a seamstress. Look who I've become! A wench! Men treat me like dirt. So when I say you're an honest man, I mean it. You are different, you are rare.

VILLON: Why did you betray your mother's dream? You could have been a wonderful seamstress.

BLANCHE: We were poor. My mother was sick. My father died when I was a child. I had a younger brother. So there was no more time for sewing or embroidering. I had to bid farewell to the dream and choose to fall.

VILLON: My Father wanted me to follow in his footsteps and become a priest.

BLANCHE: Well, isn't it almost impossible for a poor scholar of Sorbonne?

VILLON: Not if your father is the canon of the Saint-Benoit Church!

BLANCHE steps aside and gazes at VILLON amazed.

BLANCHE: How have you come to this way of life?

VILLON: That question haunts me in my worst nightmares. How? Why did I flee from my studies and books, my warm bed, my loving and kind Father Guillaume, my future? I was deceived by my own friends. They made me believe that outside, somewhere far away from the walls of the safe Saint-Benoit Church, there was freedom and real life! I decided to live the real life. Outside, on the streets. And later even outside of the Paris walls. The spring, the summer, the autumn, the winter had found me moving on, restless and dogged, trudging with my head up or down, whistling, or cursing. I have seen the life of the road and the life of the fields, waking in five hundred weary dawns to damn the birds and their infernal clatter!

BLANCHE: Seems like you didn't enjoy your freedom very much.

VILLON: Enjoy? I was trying to avoid it. I came under dukes' roofs, and I could have stayed there as a poet at Court. But after a while, the people there began poisoning me with their jealousies, their backbiting, their flattery of their patron. So I hurried away, back to my freedom! And yet every morning I wake up with a leaden heart, an aching head, an overwhelming disgust at my fate, my body, my driving passions, feeling the apathy and despair in my soul!

VILLON falls onto the bed.

BLANCHE approaches him and strokes his hair.
VILLON stands up and goes toward the door. He turns to look at BLANCHE.

VILLON: I had long fallen by the circumstances of my fate. And I blame Saturn!

BLANCHE: Are you going to chase down your freedom again?

VILLON throws a couple of coppers to the floor and exits.
    BLANCHE kneels down to pick up the money.
    VILLON comes back. He slowly opens the door and steps into the room.
    He approaches BLANCHE and helps her to get up on her feet.
    They embrace.

VILLON: We've lost our way. We've forgotten the difference between good and evil.

BLANCHE, *crying:* My mother used to punish me whenever I made a mistake.

VILLON: Whenever I was up to mischief, my Father used to lock me up in my room. But I found ways to escape from the window. Now I am going to punish myself.

BLANCHE: What do you intend to do? Where are you going?

VILLON: I am going to willingly lock myself up in a room. But this time, there will be bars instead of windows.

BLANCHE: *Prison? You are going to yield yourself prisoner?*

VILLON: I don't want this freedom anymore.

VILLON seats BLANCHE on the bed and kneels in front of her. He holds her hands in his.

BLANCHE: You cannot be serious.

VILLON: I am tired, Blanche. Tired of running. I have a feeling that I am desperately trying to run away from myself. Now, you have to fight for your future.

BLANCHE: There is no future—

VILLON: You're wrong, my dear girl. There is future. Here . . .

VILLON removes the money pouch off his belt and offers it to BLANCHE.

VILLON, *smiling:* Money doesn't prove useful when you're in prison. Take this!

BLANCHE clasps her hand to her mouth, crying. She shakes her head refusing to accept the pouch.

 VILLON puts it on the bed near her, kisses her on the forehead, and heads for the door.

BLANCHE: Thank you, Francois!

VILLON wants to turn around and look at her, but he resists his wish to do so.

 VILLON exits.

Blackout.

Scene 4

Garnier, how like you my appeal?
Did I wisely, or did I ill?
Each beast looks to his own skin's weal:
. . .Long before this I should have swung,
A scarecrow hard by Montfaucon mill!
Was it a time to hold my tongue?

July 1460. Two days later.
    Midday sun.
    The dungeon of Orleans prison.
    VILLON lies shackled on the cool stone floor of the cell. He stares at the branch of a tree that can be seen on the other side of the bars up above him.
    The branch flickers in the light breeze.

ETIENNE GARNIER, a tall burly gaoler, sits at the little lopsided table. He rolls up and unrolls a dirty scrap of paper.

VILLON sighs loudly, attracting GARNIER's attention.

VILLON: What stuffy heat! It is absolutely pointless when you are locked up inside!

VILLON moves an old tin bowl of water closer to himself with his foot. Takes a sip and spits it out onto the floor.

VILLON: This water is vile! Even rats won't drink that! Garnier? Garnier, where is my ink?

GARNIER: One is not allowed!

VILLON: Was it allowed yesterday?

VILLON grins.

VILLON: Garnier? GARNIER!

Suddenly, the great bell of the prison rings three times.
GARNIER stands up, readjusts his cloak, and sets his beret straight. He grabs a bunch of keys from the table and leaves the dungeon, closing the heavy wooden door behind him.

VILLON rises up from the floor and sits down on the bench attached to the wall. He clangs his chains and shackles and hums.

VILLON: Gallows-bird, gallows-bird, you won't fly away,
    You'll be hanged, and in Montfaucon's breeze, your body will sway . . .

The door opens, and GARNIER approaches VILLON's cell. He unlocks the door and steps in.

VILLON: Garnier, listen to this! "Francois am I, woe worth is me! At Paris born, near Pontoise citie, Whose neck, in the bight of a rope of three, Must prove how heavy my buttocks be."

VILLON laughs.
    GARNIER approaches him, grinning.

VILLON: Where is my ink? Did you bring me the ink?

GARNIER: No. Go get it yourself.

VILLON: Why?

GARNIER: Get out of here, Master Villon! Looks like your Fortune is still favorably disposed towards you!

GARNIER deals with the shackles, freeing VILLON.
    VILLON looks at him distrustfully. Then he comes down to the floor and sits in the corner of the cell.

VILLON, *sarcastically:* By all means! I intend to stay here! I am not going.

GARNIER laughs loudly and rouses VILLON up from the floor.
GARNIER clips VILLON lightly on the back of his head.

GARNIER: Muddle-head! You are being released. You've been pardoned!

VILLON: Released?

GARNIER: Hurry! We have to go outside. His Lordship Charles, the Duke of Orleans, is about to leave the prison. You must show your respect to the young Princess Marie d'Orleans. After all, you owe her your life!

VILLON: Marie . . .

VILLON's face lightens up. He squares his shoulders.

GARNIER puts his hand on VILLON's shoulder and leads him outside.

Blackout.

The prison's courtyard is flooded with sunlight.
The doors of the prison are flung open; the street is paved with strewn flowers, tapestries, and flags. The bells of Orleans are ringing.
VILLON joins the mob of former prisoners. Everyone whispers to one another.

PRISONER 1: "Joyeulx advenement! Joyeulx advenement!" The passage of a royal personage through the countryside!

PRISONER 2: Princess Marie d'Orleans delivered us due to her first entry into the capital of—

PRISONER 1: The duke's daughter?

VILLON: Yes, Marie, "O blessed birth!" I was in Blois that day in December and even drank to the newborn princess's health!

VILLON can't stop laughing. The two PRISONERS look at him mockingly.

PRISONER 2: Poor fellow! He's mad as a March hare with joy!

The DUKE OF ORLEANS and MARIE D'ORLEANS appear.

VILLON stares at them with gratitude. He hides from the mob in a nearest niche in the wall and writes down a couple of lines on a yellow paper. He throws the sheet of paper to one of the soldiers. It falls to his feet. VILLON joins the mob again and screams together with everyone else "NOEL! NOEL!"

Suddenly, a cloaked man approaches VILLON and touches him on the shoulder. VILLON turns around and is startled by the appearance of the STRANGER. His face is hidden under the cloak.

STRANGER: I am one of you. Coquille . . . I have a message for you, Michel Mouton. Paris has opened its gates for you. You can return . . .

VILLON is filled with happiness; he smiles and looks up into the clear blue sky.

When he wants to thank the STRANGER for the good news, he notices that the man has already disappeared.

Blackout.

PART 4

Scene 1

How I regret my time of May,
My days of riot, now no more,
That unperceived stole away
Till age was knocking at the door.

Paris, November 1462.

Early evening. The House of the Red Door close to the Saint-Benoit Church.

VILLON's small room in the attic.

VILLON sits, bending over the table. The room is illuminated by the single candle, standing on the windowsill before the decayed table.

VILLON coughs heavily and pulls a thick knitted gray cloak over his head. He dips his pen into the ink and starts writing some lines on a scrap of yellowed paper.

The old wooden door opens. Enter FATHER GUILLAUME DE VILLON.

VILLON doesn't hear the squeak of the closing door. He coughs violently.

FATHER GUILLAUME approaches VILLON, holding a wooden tankard in his hands. FATHER GUILLAUME puts his hand on VILLON's shoulder.

VILLON turns his head and smiles.

VILLON: Father?

The old priest smiles, puts the tankard on the table in front of VILLON, and runs his hand over VILLON's forehead.

FATHER GUILLAUME: Drink this, my son. The liquor will help. It looks like Martha is right after all. It must be a lung disease you're suffering from.

VILLON takes the tankard in his hands and smells its contents.

VILLON: What is that?

FATHER GUILLAUME: Hot mead.

VILLON takes a sip from the tankard. Puts it back on the table and turns to FATHER GUILLAUME, who sits down on the bed heavily.

FATHER GUILLAUME: Francois, what occupies your every hour? You spend all your days in seclusion. With every passing day, it seems to me that I can't recognize my cheerful, naughty, skillful fortune-hunting boy in you anymore!

VILLON: My mind is now big with my greatest work. The Testament. I am polishing my ballades, Father.

VILLON sighs, which instantly causes another bout of coughing.

VILLON: I am a tired and sick man, Father.

FATHER GUILLAUME smiles.

FATHER GUILLAUME: This statement belongs to *me* by right! You are still a young boy—

VILLON: Your boy is aging prematurely, Father. The somber years of wandering, footslogging, hunger, and prison have done their part.

FATHER GUILLAUME: Why don't you tell me what the bishop had done to you in prison? He crushed the boy I've known.

VILLON: Thibault D'Aussigny, the bishop of Meun! Why don't we say his name out loud? Oh, heartless swine! "A summer's tide on crusts I pined and water cold by his decree. He starved me sorely, harsh or kind. God be to him as he to me." God, be to him as he to me!

VILLON buries his face in his hands and lets out a sob.

—

74

FATHER GUILLAUME rises hastily and approaches VILLON. The priest folds VILLON in his arms.

FATHER GUILLAUME: Don't tempt the Lord! Be grateful, my son. You are free, our Savior has forgiven your sins and gifted you a new life. A chance to have a fresh start!

FATHER GUILLAUME crosses himself.

FATHER GUILLAUME: Francois, I am proud that you've become an educated man. Our Lord has endowed you with a variety of skills and extensive knowledge! Why don't you bring some happiness to your old Father Guillaume and promise to share your blessed gifts with others? I can help you find some pupils—

VILLON: Father, I have tasted the humiliation in full. I am an ideal tutor neither in appearance nor in reputation . . . Absolutely everyone in our old Paris City knows about my . . . adventures . . . with the guards, in prisons. Your pupils will make a laughingstock of me!

VILLON stands up and makes his way toward an old wooden chest in the dark corner of the room. He throws it open, kneels down, and starts searching for something, retrieving moldering wooden tablets with inscriptions on them.
  FATHER GUILLAUME comes closer to VILLON and, raising the hem of his long black soutane, sits down on the other chest, which stands near the door. He watches VILLON.
  VILLON pulls out a pile of yellowed paper that is tied up with a cord. He laughs.

VILLON: Father, I have found it! Here!

VILLON springs to his feet. His eyes light up.
  VILLON sits down beside FATHER GUILLAUME and solemnly offers the pile of papers to him.

VILLON: Here! I want you to have it, Father! This is my early work. I want you to keep the best of me! Do you remember the riot of the *Pet-au-Diable*? It inspired me for the first time, and I wrote this long ballade.

VILLON laughs and immediately coughs.

FATHER GUILLAUME: You have a magic touch in poetry, my son.

VILLON takes FATHER GUILLAUME's hand in his and rests his head on FATHER's shoulder.

VILLON: I give you my word, Father. I know what I should do! I can become a copyist to one of the guild of scriveners in the quarter, on the Rue des Parcheminiers. I will go there right now!

VILLON jumps to his feet and throws the cloak upon his shoulders.
    FATHER GUILLAUME stands in the doorway, blocking VILLON's way.

FATHER GUILLAUME: Francois! You don't feel well. It's too late and dark outside. Why don't you stay at home, and we will have a delicious supper together? We will open the new bottle of Beaune. We will have a fatted goose stuffed and roasted. And your dear old mother will be joining us!

VILLON: Father, do not worry so much! I am less than ever inclined to seek out trouble! I will keep an eye on the tavern door and dexterously fleet away when a brawl arises and the women begin to scream for the watch!

FATHER GUILLAUME approaches VILLON.

FATHER GUILLAUME: My son, you are going to a tavern? Alone?

VILLON: Robin Dogis invited me for supper. We will be in the Chariot.

FATHER GUILLAUME feels sad and lowers his gaze. He nods to his thought.
    VILLON approaches FATHER GUILLAUME and embraces him.

VILLON: We will have our supper tomorrow, I promise. I will stay at home tomorrow, and I bet you will grow tired of my foolish twaddle soon enough!

FATHER GUILLAUME: I have been missing your foolish twaddle for so many years!

VILLON goes to the bed and takes the pouch of money from under his pillow.
    VILLON playfully shoves the pouch under his beret. He smiles.

VILLON: Tomorrow! I promise!

FATHER GUILLAUME: Much water can flow under the bridge until tomorrow.

VILLON: But you will reserve some Beaune for me.

FATHER GUILLAUME: Now I do recognize my little stubborn boy! Francois, please be careful! Tomorrow may turn out to be quite different from what you expect.

VILLON: Father, nothing will be different tomorrow! The reckless adventures of Francois Villon are over! I will not exchange the roof over my head, the warm bed in the attic, certainty of a dinner, and your blessed company and love for anything else in the whole universe!

FATHER GUILLAUME, *laughing softly* : Lord, have mercy! Let's hope so!

FATHER GUILLAUME lets VILLON pass through the door.
VILLON turns round and smiles.

VILLON: I love you, Father! Swear to be careful and obedient. After the tavern, I am coming home right away. You will be still awake, and I will come to your room to wish you a blessed and peaceful night, and you will grant me absolution once again!

FATHER GUILLAUME makes a sign of the cross over VILLON.
VILLON smiles again and exits.

FATHER GUILLAUME, *calling after Villon:* LET THE LOVE OF GOD OUR SAVIOR LEAD YOU! AND YOUR OLD FATHER LOVES YOU, FRANCOIS! PLEASE, RETURN BEFORE MIDNIGHT!

The muffled voices and recessive footsteps can be heard coming from the street.
FATHER GUILLAUME sighs, goes up to the table, and looks intently at the burning candle.

FATHER GUILLAUME: Well, some things don't change much after all. Not in eight years even . . .

FATHER GUILLAUME blows out the candle.
He exits the room in twilight, whispering the words of prayer on his way.

Blackout.

Scene 2

The Stabbing of Master Francois Ferrebourg

That same night.

The Rue des Parcheminiers is plunged into darkness. It is illuminated only by the candlelight, flickering in occasional windows.

High overhanging eaves and gables cast peculiar shadows.

A broad splash of light pours across the cobbles from the open window of the house at the sign of the Keg, next door to the Mule tavern.

Another sign can be seen on the same house swinging in the wind that reads: Master Ferrebourg's Scriptorium.

The clerks sit toiling over some urgent piece of law-writing inside the house.

VILLON and his three half-tipsy companions return from the Chariot tavern.

They stumble along the street, caterwaul loudly, and burst out laughing.

VILLON supports ROBIN DOGIS, and they gaily sing a raucous song.

VILLON and ROBIN:

> "Jenin l'Avenu,
> Quick, while the baths are hot,
> Go, get a scrub, shoo!
> Jenin l'Avenu . . ."

ROGER PICHART and HUTIN DU MOUSTIER follow, arguing and gaily ripping off curses.

ROGER: Hutin, you old fart! Jeanette is young enough to be your granddaughter! (*He belches, laughs.*)

HUTIN: Jeanette gave *me* a wink first! You know what they have in mind when they (*He winks*) and I was about to follow her into the wench's room, but *you* showed up from nowhere! And what was that whispering about? (*He mimics a passionate whisper.*) "Jeanetton, why don't you rest your hand on my pouch? You don't want anyone to steal it from you, do you?"

ROGER squints and grins.

ROGER: I didn't exactly mean the pouch on my belt . . . She is not as naive as you are! And she knows what I like.

HUTIN: You, dirty scum!

ROGER: Hold your horses! I wonder what you were expecting to get in the wench's room!

ROGER halts by the window of the Ferrebourg's Scriptorium.

Archly watches the clerks at work and spits through the window, aiming at one of them.

ROGER: HEY, BASTARDS! YES, YOU! WORKING SO LATE, THINK OF YOUR POOR WIVES SLEEPING IN THEIR COLD BEDS! HA, OR THEY HAVE FOUND SOMEONE TO REPLACE YOU AT NIGHT!

HUTIN: Roger! Quit taunting the clerks!

ROGER: BASTARDS! What, you want a fight? Wish to buy any flutes as we call it?

HUTIN grabs ROGER's hand and attempts to drag him away from the window. ROGER resists, bends down, picks up a stone, and throws it into the window. He tears his hand out of HUTIN's grasp and approaches the window once again.
     The CLERKS, outraged by such behavior, dash into the street. They peer into the dark.

CLERK 1: What ruffians are these?

CLERK 2: Look, there they are!

VILLON and ROBIN stand still near the Mule tavern. VILLON clings fast to the wall and tries to hide his face in the shadows.

ROBIN: Hey, the attractive frolic is about to develop into trouble!
Let's join our friends!

VILLON: Robin! Wait! Don't! Please don't! (*He whispers.*) I have seen enough trouble.

VILLON tries to hold ROBIN back, but it's too late, and ROBIN joins the unfolding brawl.
VILLON stays where he is.

Meanwhile, the CLERKS scuffle with ROGER and HUTIN. Loud oaths resound along the street.
One of the clerks punches ROGER in the face, and ROGER falls to the ground.
HUTIN attacks the assaulter, springs up on his back, and tries to throttle him.
The CLERK throws HUTIN down to the ground and screams, hitting him with his iron candlestick.
The other two clerks approach HUTIN. They roughly capture him and take into the house of Master FERREBOURG.

HUTIN, *screams:* MURDER! MURDER! THEY ARE KILLING ME!

CLERK 2: We'll hand him over to the watch! Lock him up!

HUTIN: I AM DEAD!

ROBIN runs after the clerks.

ROBIN: HUTIN! I'll save you!

As the CLERKS drag HUTIN into the house, Master FERREBOURG, having heard the loud noises and screams coming from outside, runs out into the street.
FERREBOURG gives ROBIN a strong shove that sends him sprawling across the pavement.

ROBIN stands up, whips out his dagger, and furiously aims a flying stab at FERREBOURG.

FERREBOURG: What in the world?

FERREBOURG is wounded. He clasps his bleeding shoulder and tries to catch ROBIN. But he is too weak, and he is losing blood, so FERREBOURG leans against the wall of the house.

FERREBOURG: Stupid scoundrels! I know who you are! You will end up on the gallows in no time! I have friends in Châtelet!

ROBIN, *shouts to ROGER:* RUN! TO THE CLOISTER, YOU CAN CLAIM SANCTUARY THERE! RUN!

ROBIN and ROGER disappear into the dark.

VILLON, who has been hiding in the shadows during the brawl, attempts to escape. He slips into the nearest street, leading to the Saint-Benoit Church.

FERREBOURG turns around and catches sight of VILLON's face right at the moment the unbiased spectator turns tail to fly.

Blackout.

Later that night.

VILLON slinks like a cat by shortcuts home, to the safety of the Red Door.

VILLON rushes into the house.

FATHER GUILLAUME comes downstairs, holding a candle in his hands.

VILLON closes the door behind him and leans against it, breathing heavily.

FATHER GUILLAUME approaches VILLON.

VILLON: Good night, Father!

FATHER GUILLAUME: Francois! What has happened? You are out of breath.

VILLON throws himself into FATHER GUILLAUME's arms, sobs.

VILLON: Father, pardon my voluntary and involuntary sins, known and unknown, in mind and thought! Forgive me for leaving the house tonight!

FATHER GUILLAUME: Our Lord will absolve your sins, my boy! Calm down, calm down and tell me what happened.

VILLON draws back and smiles at FATHER GUILLAUME.

VILLON: A misfortunate evening, my Father!

VILLON sighs, lowers his eyes, and wends his way to his room in the attic.
He walks up three steps, turns round, and looks at FATHER GUILLAUME.
FATHER GUILLAUME locks the door and leans against it. They silently look at each other.

VILLON: Father, I love you.

FATHER GUILLAUME, *smiling:* I love you as well, my boy! Go and take a good rest.

VILLON: Can we have a dinner together, with my mother, tomorrow? Just like you mentioned before?

FATHER GUILLAUME: I will order Martha to stuff the goose.

VILLON reaches the door to his room and stops dead.
The tramp of archers coming up the cloister of Saint-Benoit is heard. They halt at the door.
He hears a knock on the door.

ARCHER: In the name of the provost of Paris, open the door!

FATHER GUILLAUME opens the door. The archers burst into the house and seize VILLON.

FATHER GUILLAUME: Monsignor, what are you doing? I earnestly ask you to let my son go!

ARCHER: Father, your son has been present at the locus delicti! He will be thrust into Châtelet with the others.

FATHER GUILLAUME: Others? What crime?

ARCHER: The stabbing of Master Francois Ferrebourg!

VILLON tries to break loose from the archers. But they hold him fast.
VILLON looks at FATHER GUILLAUME beggarly.

VILLON, *crying:* Father, Father, I had no share in tonight's brawl whatsoever! I had no part in the insulting of Master Ferrebourg!

The archers tie VILLON up and take him away from the house.
FATHER GUILLAUME follows the violent procession. He brushes away his tears that trickle down the wrinkled, disappointed face of the old man.

FATHER GUILLAUME: Be brave, my Francois! It must be a mistake! Be brave!

The procession exits.
FATHER GUILLAUME walks slowly toward the House of the Red Door, praying.

Blackout.

Scene 3

God knows I shall not dread the tomb
When all my merry times are flown.

Late evening of December 30, 1462.

One of the cells in prison Châtelet.
    The cell is illuminated by just two candles. Cold wind roars outside.

VILLON, chained up, lies on a rusty iron bench.

Enter Lieutenant PIERRE DE LA DEHORS with GUARDS.
    The GUARDS remain by the cell's door.
    At the sound of the opening door, VILLON half-rises.
    DE LA DEHORS approaches VILLON.

DE LA DEHORS: Well, well, well! We've met again. What a nice place for a meeting, don't you think?

VILLON: Pierre, Pierre De La Dehors? You haven't changed a bit! Just as you were back in students' years in Sorbonne. You were that thoughtless chappie who loved hanging about in the Mule with—

DE LA DEHORS, *irritated:* Don't! Don't rake over old ashes, Villon! There is no time like the present. Present is precious! Look at us. You are a miserable rat chained up! (*He grins.*) And I turned out to be a lieutenant of Paris. I imprisoned you! (*Maliciously*) Not bad for a "thoughtless chappie," ha?

DE LA DEHORS paces up and down the cell.

DE LA DEHORS: Yes, there is no time like the present. Review your past, present, and *immediate* future now, Villon! You may not be given a chance to do so betimes! You, uncatchable gaolbird! Look, you have come to be in the claws of justice once again, and this time, you are not going to slip through our fingers!

DE LA DEHORS emits a short dismaying laugh.

VILLON, *stands up resolutely:* What do you want from me, Pierre? I ran away the moment the trouble began. You cannot hang me for that, can you? I had had no part in the insulting of the clerks, the brawl that followed, or the stabbing!

DE LA DEHORS, *stops in the opposite corner of the cell:* Oh, I guess, you know what I want. No one is overjoyed to see you here. No one expected your return. There is nothing for you here in Paris, Villon! Except for stone-cold walls of the cell, dirty stinking water, and gallows. It is a terrible mistake you've made coming back, Villon! Did you really think that nothing changed during those years? Did you think that people in the Prosecutor's General Office and the Supreme Court had forgotten about your "misadventures"? Is that how you call it?

VILLON: I feel deep sympathy for you, Pierre! Through all these years you haven't been able to enjoy your life, you've wasted each and every day chasing the facts and rumors about my adventures! It couldn't have been easy to frame up a case against me!

DE LA DEHORS, *grinds his teeth with satisfaction:* Oh, on the contrary, it's impossible to lose track of you! Dens, fights, brigandism! No one forgot how on one lovely summer night you robbed the church!

VILLON leans against the wall.

VILLON: Really? Is that what you wanted to talk to me about?

DE LA DEHORS: You believe I have forgotten all about the affray with the butchers and the theft of hooks during the *Pet-au-Diable* celebrations all those years ago?

VILLON licks his dry lips, smiles spitefully.

VILLON: Admit it, Pierre, you have never had so much fun in your tedious life! You could have joined the celebrations!

DE LA DEHORS darts a furious look at VILLON and slowly approaches him.

DE LA DEHORS: Never. I would never mingle with the crowd of dirty scholars! You are a clerk of University and therefore my enemy.

VILLON: Bi God! You were a scholar yourself! And now what, you are denying your past?

VILLON notices an ominous glitter in DE LA DEHORS's eyes.
DE LA DEHORS stares fixedly at VILLON and hisses like a snake.

DE LA DEHORS: Listen to me very carefully. Right now, you are not in a position to talk or philosophize about my past! You will be dangling on the gallows tomorrow morning! You know why? Not only because the case of the church robbery is not closed yet. You even got away with the murder of the priest! No, not this time, Villon!

DE LA DEHORS pulls out a little wooden box from his cloak.
VILLON gasps for air. His eyes fixed on the wooden box. He tries to reach it with his hand, but the chains won't let him do that.

VILLON: My box of poems! You stole it! Scoundrel! Brute!

DE LA DEHORS sits down on the iron bench, attached to the opposite wall of the cell, holding the box. Then he bends forward and places the box on the floor, in the middle of the cell.
VILLON tries to reach it again, but his chains won't let him.

DE LA DEHORS: You have bad luck choosing friends, Villon! Tabarie . . . I see you remember him, blurted out your name at the questioning. And Laurens passed *this* to me.

VILLON: Laurens! You bribed him!

DE LA DEHORS: You don't know how much I had to pay to get hold of it! Most of your friends, rascals, are waiting for you as ghosts around the corner, and others are just . . . traitors?

DE LA DEHORS smiles viciously.
VILLON hangs down his head and rocks himself to and fro.

DE LA DEHORS: Oh, believe me, it will be worth it when I lay your ballads open to the public! Disparagement of executive government, insulting, disgusting verses about people from high society!

VILLON, *laughs*: The public has been singing my ballads in every tavern, heard it all around Paris! Bravo, Pierre! Finally my words have reached your ears!

DE LA DEHORS hits VILLON. He falls to his knees.

DE LA DEHORS: Words! Stupid, rude, vulgar, vile words!

DE LA DEHORS squats down. He faces VILLON.

DE LA DEHORS: I want you out of the way once and for all! You are the most troublesome blackguard, a rioter, burglar, assassin, robber of churches, you belong to the most desperate gang of villains! Do you honestly think that your dossier will not be sufficient a reason to condemn you to death? Oh, but I am a loyal and kind man. I can help you. If you leave Paris tonight and swear not to come back ever again. But . . . before that . . . you will publicly ask for forgiveness in front of all the people that you wrote about.

VILLON, *ferociously:* Really? This is an intolerable injustice! You cannot hang me for my ballads!

DE LA DEHORS: What are you whispering there?

VILLON: My poems! I will never be able to write ballads such as these again . . . They are my past, my future!

DE LA DEHORS: Do not worry, I will cover your path to Montfaucon with your precious ballads with my own hands!

DE LA DEHORS stands up and goes to the iron-barred window.

DE LA DEHORS, *floutingly:* God blessed you with talent, Villon! How do you rhyme those words? Your ballads are good, really good. Maybe I won't use them against you in your case. There is enough evidence to hang you. I will keep your little wooden box! But tell me, how do you write them? Where do you find the words?

VILLON: Everywhere. On the walls, on the streets, in the faces, in my heart. You will never understand it! My ballads belong just to me!

DE LA DEHORS, *angrily:* Idiot! Cretin! Nothing belongs to you anymore, not even your own miserable life!

VILLON: I despise you!

DE LA DEHORS, *floutingly:* Leave Paris once and for all, vanish! What are you going to choose, you loathsome scribbler—life and freedom, or death? Because if you stay, I will talk to the hangman Kiddy and tell him to be generous to you and get a firm rope.

VILLON spits into DE LA DEHORS's face.
    DE LA DEHORS wipes his face.

VILLON sits down on the bench.

VILLON: Just go to hell!

DE LA DEHORS is in a frenzy of rage.

DE LA DEHORS: You'll pay for your "misadventures"! That will be an unforgettable show! You see, the king is not likely to die again to oblige you. The little princess will not save your buttocks! You will finally feel the jerk of the cart pulling from underneath, hear the thick choke, writhe in convulsions, and I will enjoy your final grimace, *la moe!* You will dangle there and rot, rain will wash your bones, sun will dry and blacken your skin, the birds will peck out your eyes, and all the toughs of Paris will bring their wenches out to laugh at you! Your friends, Colin, Montigny have already become rattling bags of bones, and they are waiting for you to join them!

VILLON, *choking:* Who did no wrong need not confess. It's absurd! You cannot hang me just for your own amusement!

DE LA DEHORS, *screams to the guards:* Take him into the Chamber of Question, force him again to the agonizing water treatments, make him vomit and scream in agony! I will prepare the documents required for condemnation followed by *extreme sentence.*

VILLON curls up on the iron bench. He shivers violently, whispering.

VILLON: This is the end! This is the end!

DE LA DEHORS: Bravo, Villon! This *is* the end!

A sudden downpour of rain can be heard outside.
VILLON sobs.

DE LA DEHORS: Poet! Saturn has played you his last trick. You are to be hanged. Can you smell the stench of the nearing death?

DE LA DEHORS turns away with disgust and fingers the jewel at his neck.

DE LA DEHORS: Poet, listen, the sky is paying its last tribute to you!

VILLON shakes. The tears run down his frightened face.

DE LA DEHORS: Tomorrow we shall hear you squeak a pretty song before long!

DE LA DEHORS laughs, and the stone gray walls of the cell echo back his uncontrollable laughter.

DE LA DEHORS exits.
The moment the door of the cell closes, the loud noise of hurried footsteps can be heard coming from the passage.
A loud screechy voice screams, "Monsignor! Lieutenant De La Dehors! Come to the Court please. The Court has reconsidered the case of Master . . ."

VILLON holds his breath. He retrieves a yellowed scrap of paper from behind one of the wall stones. Bends over it, scribbling a poem.
The rain lessens, and the first bashful rays of sun struggle through the clouds, lighting up the cell.

Blackout.

Scene 4

Farewell, I say, with tearful eye.

Three days later.

Late afternoon of January 3, 1463.

The crossroad near the House of the Red Door. Candle light glows in every window of the house, making it look as if the inhabitants of the house are getting ready for a feast.

A young gangly LAD in a green beret aslant passes by the House, holding a scroll before him. The LAD cries in a loud and breaking voice.

LAD: Attention! The Court having considered the case brought by the provost of Paris and his lieutenant against Master Francois Villon, and the latter having appealed from the sentence of hanging and strangling. It is finally ordered that the said appeal, and the sentence preceding, be annulled, and having regard to the bad character of the said Villon, that he be banished for ten years from the Town, Provosty, and Viscounty of Paris! (*Clears his throat.*) Attention! Attention! Townspeople must not receive, comfort, nor aid in any way the said Villon.

The LAD disappears around the corner.

Blackout.

The House of the Red Door.

The overhanging cloud of sorrow fills the room.

FATHER GUILLAUME stands at the dining table, fussing over the bundle for VILLON.

His servant MARTHA wraps up some pasties.

In the far end of the room sits a stooped old woman, Villon's MOTHER, neatly folding up some well-worn clothes.

VILLON enters, stops by the fireplace, and looks at the fire.

Then he approaches FATHER GUILLAUME and puts his hand on the priest's shoulder.

FATHER GUILLAUME turns his head, looks at VILLON, and forces a smile.

FATHER GUILLAUME: I am gathering a little bundle for your journey. (*Turns to look at Martha.*) Martha, pass me that bottle of Beaune, will you?

MARTHA gives the bottle of wine to FATHER GUILLAUME, who holds it in front of himself, and pats the old bottle.

FATHER GUILLAUME: Here, your favorite wine, my boy. I have saved it for you. Since we never had our dinner together and, who knows, maybe we never will . . . (*His voice breaks.*) Here, you will drink it on your own and think of us.

VILLON: I don't need wine to think of you, Father. I will always think of you.

VILLON gives FATHER an encouraging smile.

VILLON: I know that *you* were the one who saved my buttocks once again. You have set in motion every influence you could come at, every legal and parliamentary influence.

FATHER GUILLAUME: I love you, Francois. And I will do everything in my power for you, everything in my power to protect you.

VILLON presses his face against FATHER's shoulder.

VILLON, *with an affected cheerfulness:* I will be back soon, Father. The time is in the habit of flying by so quickly, isn't it? And after all, what is ten years' banishment when the neck is safe?

FATHER GUILLAUME slowly nods his head and rubs his forehead.

FATHER GUILLAUME: Of course, Francois, you will be back soon.

FATHER GUILLAUME tousles VILLON's hair.

FATHER GUILLAUME: I thank our Lord that you were granted the three days' grace. Although they will confiscate everything you have—

VILLON: They have nothing to confiscate from me, for I don't have any property, and the only worthwhile thing I have got (*nods toward the box of poems that he holds in his hands*) I am leaving behind. I give it to you. My poems are the very best of me, Father. I want you to keep them safe.

FATHER GUILLAUME takes the wooden box and puts it on the table in front of him.

FATHER GUILLAUME: Can I read them?

VILLON: Yes, my Father. And you know, maybe one day I will become a well-known poet and people will say "Ah, this is poet Villon's ballad. The one who was Guillaume de Villon's son!"

VILLON laughs softly.
    FATHER smiles and slightly pushes VILLON toward his MOTHER.

FATHER GUILLAUME: Go, sit with her.

VILLON: I don't have much clothes, and she is still folding.

FATHER GUILLAUME: We all have different ways of hiding our grief. I am sorry to tell you that . . . Francois, go up to your mother. She will probably never see her son again on this earth.

VILLON lowers his eyes. He slightly moves away from FATHER GUILLAUME and turns to look at his MOTHER.
    FATHER squeezes VILLON's shoulder.

VILLON, *whispers:* I can't face her, Father. I can't watch the constant tears running down her cheeks.

FATHER GUILLAUME: It will hurt even more if you don't spend these last moments with her.

VILLON: How dared I desert her in the past?

VILLON approaches his MOTHER in a heavy tread.
 The old woman holds up her head. VILLON sees her tearstained face.
 MOTHER smiles faintly.
 VILLON falls to his knees and clasps his mother's knees tight.
 MOTHER puts her hand on his head.

MOTHER: Just like you used to do as a child.

VILLON: Please forgive me, Mother! I love you, and you have always been the only human being who loved me, with all my faults and mistakes. Please forgive me, I should have stayed at home, and we could have had our dinner *together*!

MOTHER, *tears running down her cheeks:* My little boy, don't regret anything. Everything happens for a reason. It was not meant to be.

VILLON, *sobs:* I am not worthy of you!

MOTHER: God knows better. We are worthy of everything we get in this life. And I have been blessed with a kind, loving, talented son (*overcoming the burr in her throat*) who loved adventures.

VILLON: Stupid son!

MOTHER: Not for me.

MOTHER raises his chin up with her hand and kisses his forehead.
 VILLON sits next to her, and they embrace.
 MOTHER cries and clasps her child tightly in her arms, as though wishing to shelter him from the entire world.

MOTHER: I will always be waiting for you. Wherever you are, know that I am here, waiting for my little boy, and my prayers will be paving the way for you. I am waiting for you here. And when I die, just think of me, and I will live in your memories and your heart.

VILLON, *despairingly:* Mother!

MOTHER cradles VILLON's head against the deflated remains of her breast. And rocks to and fro.

MOTHER: That's how life is. Remember me, and that will mean that I was once here.

FATHER GUILLAUME approaches them.

FATHER GUILLAUME: Francois, it's time.

VILLON stands up heavily, helps his MOTHER to her feet.
    MOTHER leans on the arm of FATHER GUILLAUME.
    MARTHA closes the procession. She helps VILLON toss the bundle on his shoulder.
    They silently come nearer to the door.
    VILLON stops, opens the door, and turns about.
    FATHER GUILLAUME thrusts a purse into VILLON's hand. They embrace.
    The stooping old priest in his black cloak stands in the open doorway of the House of the Red Door, blessing the wonderer for the last time with the cross.

Long embrace. FATHER mutters the last benedictions over VILLON's head.

VILLON embraces his MOTHER. She stands still, pressing her son to her.
    FATHER GUILLAUME and MARTHA draw the trembling old woman in tears aside.
    VILLON brushes the tears from his face, gives a farewell wink to MARTHA, who cries holding her hand over her mouth.
    VILLON walks slouching down the street, leaving the old woman and the priest blind with tears on the threshold of the House of the Red Door.

VILLON walks past the place where the priest Chermoye had fallen, past the house of Master de Vaucelles. He lingers for a moment and watches the house.

VILLON, *exhales:* Katherine! Farewell with heavy heart say I . . .

VILLON keeps on walking. He passes the stone bench under the clock of Saint-Benoit Church, where he had sat that night of Corpus Christi. His heart sinks, and he stands still. He notices a female figure sitting on the bench.
    VILLON takes a breath and comes closer to the woman hesitantly, peering into the darkness.

The woman hears the footsteps and faces him. She slowly rises.
VILLON drops his bundle to the ground.

VILLON: ISABEL!

ISABEL takes off from the place near the bench and flings herself swiftly into VILLON's arms.

Tears run down her rose-petal cheeks.
They stand still, huddling together like two sparrows on a rainy day.

ISABEL, *sobbing:* I knew I'd see you again!

VILLON strokes her hair.

VILLON: Isabel, my dear Isabel!

ISABEL: I have been waiting for all these years to tell you . . . I have always loved you.

VILLON: I have been constantly seeing this moment in my dreams.

ISABEL lovingly presses her finger to his lips.

ISABEL: Let me speak, my darling!

They approach the bench and sit down embracing each other.
ISABEL examines VILLON's face. She touches the scar on his upper lip.

ISABEL: That scar!

They kiss humbly.

ISABEL: I have always loved you, Francois. People say there can be only one true love in your life. You were mine. And despite that I am married and I have children now, my love has never faded away. It burns within me like eternal fire. I was waiting for you every day, looking out of the window, whenever a wobbly man in a black cloak passed beneath my window. I live waiting breathlessly, and this waiting was giving me life. (*She caresses his face.*) I will be waiting.

ISABEL's voice breaks, and she cries silently.

They embrace.

VILLON: Isabel, Isabel. I come to understand it just now—the melody of your name has always been hidden some place safe in my heart. Here (*gives her a little yellowed piece of paper*) I have once written these lines for a newly married gentleman. I know that a poet cannot write a word on the paper if it doesn't mean a thing to him personally. I know now as I knew then somewhere deep inside my heart, but was too slow and late to realize what I knew . . . I am not making any sense, am I? (*He gives her an apologetic smile.*) This was meant for you . . . . *Princesse?*

ISABEL takes the piece of paper, unfolds it, and reads.

VILLON: "My princess, these resolves of mine ensure
　　　　My heart will never part from your heart, whether
　　　　Come weal or woe: grant me a love as pure,
　　　　E'en for this end we are alone together."

ISABEL cries. They embrace and stay like that. She squeezes the piece of paper in her hand.

ISABEL: Where are you heading?

VILLON, *laughs softly:* Are you going to follow me?

ISABEL: I will always follow you, secretly, and maybe someday, I will find you in Orleans . . .

VILLON: Poitou.

ISABEL: Is that where you are going?

VILLON: Yes. The time has come for a fresh start. In every human nature, the fine and the gross exist coupled with one another, constantly fighting. I have succumbed to the gross so many times in my life. It has always seemed to be stronger than me. I mean that part of myself. But now, God has granted me another chance, a new life. It is time to find myself at last! I am retiring to Saint-Maixent in Poitou. My maternal uncle is the good honest abbot of that place.

ISABEL: Then you are going to lose your freedom. Freedom that has always been so important to you. It has been your only way of existence. You have been chasing your freedom through all these years, outside of Paris, during your wanderings. Fighting for it!

VILLON: I am tired of that freedom, Isabel. It is not easy to admit, but because of that stupid chase, I have lost everything.

ISABEL: Will you be able to live without adventures?

VILLON, *shrugging his shoulders:* Maybe the monkhood was meant to be the main adventure of my life. And I ran away from it and hid myself in taverns!

VILLON smiles bitterly.
    ISABEL pats his hand.

ISABEL: Francois, can a poet of your stature, knowing all the things you have written, feeling your mastery, just stop writing?

VILLON peers into the darkness in front of him. Then he looks at the track of moonlight that lies at ISABEL's feet.
    VILLON sighs.

VILLON: I will never be able to stifle the voice within me. I want to write a Mystery.

VILLON rises up to his feet and picks up his bundle.
    ISABEL follows him.

ISABEL: I promise to visit your mother as often as possible—

VILLON hangs his head. His eyes fill with tears.

VILLON: My mother, (*his voice breaks*) my poor old mother!

ISABEL embraces him. She helps VILLON put the bundle over his shoulder.

ISABEL: I will be recounting the stories of your adventures to her, set her mind at rest, by telling her that you are all right.

VILLON: I thank you, my faithful guardian angel! Please, guard my mother.

ISABEL smiles. She folds the yellow piece of paper that she has been holding in her hand and puts it into a small locket around her neck.
ISABEL kisses VILLON. They embrace.

VILLON turns to go. He moves away. Suddenly turns around and looks at ISABEL, standing at the church.

ISABEL: I will see you again, my love!

VILLON disappears into the darkness.
VILLON passes Sorbonne. Stops for a moment, then kicks a cobble with his foot and keeps on walking.
He pulls his hood well over his eyes and passes under the massive stone arch of the Saint Jacques Gate, which is flanked by two round towers.
The guard paces above.
VILLON crosses the bridge over the moat. He turns round and watches the gates and the sleeping city perdu on the other side of the stone wall.
The melancholy overcomes his tired spirit and body.

VILLON: For the last time. I want to remember you just like that, city of my youth, my follies, my love and disappointment. Each corner of yours holds a memory. My Paris, keep my memories forever. And don't forget your prodigal son, your poor scholar Villon!

VILLON heaves a groan and walks away. He trudges off along the southern road once more.
VILLON vanishes into the gathering January darkness.

Eternal rest be his for aye
In clear and everlasting light.

Repos eternel donne a cil,
Sire, et clarte perpetuelle.

Quotations Used in Parts 1 and 2

I know all save myself alone.

The Complete Poems of Francois Villon / The Testaments of Francois Villon. Translated by John Heron Lepper, including the texts of John Payne and others. Horace Liveright Inc., Liveright Publishing Corporation, USA, 1924.

Divers poems. Ballad of things known and unknown. Page 277, line 8.

Part 1. Scene 2

> **1. Mad hearts of youth where wisdom's snows**
> **Yet never fell. Alack, 'tis truth!**
> **But they who be my fiercest foes**
> **Don't wish me to outlive my youth.**

The Completed Poems of Francois Villon / The Testaments of Francois Villon.

Translated by John Heron Lepper, including texts of John Payne and others. Liveright Publishing Corporation, 1924, Horace Liveright Inc., New York.

The Great Testament, page 20. Stanza XV (starting from fifth line).

2. Qui m'a este plus doux que mere

101

Francois Villon. *Oeuvres*. Editions Garnier Freres, 6, Rue des Saints-Peres, Paris. 1962

Le Testament. LXXXVII, page 58 (line 3).

Part 1. Scene 3.

> **1. My clerks, like bird-lime gripping all,**
> **When out upon the prigging lay**
> **Or robbing, watch your skins I pray:**
> **For following these pastimes twain**
> **Colin de Cayeulx had to pay.**

The Completed Poems of Francois Villon / The Testaments of Francois Villon.

Translated by John Heron Lepper, including texts of John Payne and others. Liveright Publishing Corporation, 1924, Horace Liveright Inc., New York.

The Great Testament, page 85. "Villon's Good Counsel to the Forlorn Hope" (starting from third line).

2. So nimble, and so full of subtle flame, As if that every one from whence they came . . . Had meant to put his whole wit in a jest.

Francois Villon: A Documented Survey by D. B. Wyndham Lewis. With a preface by Hilaire Belloc. The Literary Guild of America. 1928. Coward-MC Cann Inc. Printed and bound by J. J. Little and Ives Company, New York, USA.

The line from the *Metamorphoses*. Part the Life. Page 86.

Part 1. Scene 4.

1. KILL! KILL! SAVE THE SOW! KILL! KILL! SAVE THE SOW!

Francois Villon: A Documented Survey by D. B. Wyndham Lewis. 1928 by Coward-MC Cann Inc. Printed and bound by J. J. Little and Ives Company, New York, USA.

The Life. §2. Page 93.

Part 2. Scene 1.

> **1. Harsh justice his behind did flay**
> **And make him seek in exile flight;**
> **In vain' twas: "I appeal" to say,**
> **A law term no too recondite.**
> **Eternal rest be his for aye.**

The Completed Poems of Francois Villon / The Testaments of Francois Villon.

Translated by John Heron Lepper, including texts of John Payne and others. Liveright Publishing Corporation, 1924, Horace Liveright Inc., New York.

The Great Testament. Rondeau (that follows the stanza CLXV, from the eighth line), page 95.

2. The many-colored procession of Corpus Christi passes through the streets, the children strew the flowers around, the white-robed singing-men raise a loud song, servers bear lighted candles and flaming wax torches, the thurifers with silver censers toss clouds of white fragrant smoke into the summer air, more lights, more singers, more friars and monks and beadles appear in the streets and the populace joins and follows the Sacred Host in its precious monstrance born by the celebrating priests under a canopy rich with cloth of gold and tassels, the bells ring and the chanting.

Francois Villon: A Documented Survey by D. B. Wyndham Lewis. 1928 by Coward-MC Cann Inc. Printed and bound by J. J. Little and Ives Company, New York, USA.

The Life. § 2. Page 108-09.

3. CHERMOYE: By God! I have found you!
VILLON: Have I wronged you?

Francois Villon: A Documented Survey by D. B. Wyndham Lewis. 1928 by Coward-MC Cann Inc. Printed and bound by J. J. Little and Ives Company, New York, USA.

The Life. § 3. Page 110.

Registers of the Chancellery of France, JJ 187 (149, fol. 76v).

Part 2. Scene 2.

> **1. They cannot blame me justly here,**
> **Except that others paid too dear.**
> **I tell the truth and nothing less,**
> **And speak this boast with conscience clear;**
> **Who did no wrong need not confess.**

The Completed Poems of Francois Villon / The Testaments of Francois Villon.

Translated by John Heron Lepper, including texts of John Payne and others. Liveright Publishing Corporation, 1924, Horace Liveright Inc., New York.

The Great Testament. Stanza XXIV (starting from the fourth line), page 23.

Part 2. Scene 3.

> **1. This danger to escape, I trow,**
> **The best plan is to run away.**
> **Adieu! I'm off to Angers now.**

The Completed Poems of Francois Villon / The Testaments of Francois Villon.

Translated by John Heron Lepper, including texts of John Payne and others. Liveright Publishing Corporation, 1924, Horace Liveright Inc., New York.

The Little Testament. Stanza VI, page 4.

> **2. Had I but studied hard, in truth,**
> **When I was young, nor played the fool,**
> **But been a very virtuous youth,**
> **I'd have a house and lie in wool.**
> **But ah! I ran away from school,**
> **A way that naughty children take.**
> **The words are written; with the dule**
> **Indeed my heart is like to break.**

The Completed Poems of Francois Villon / The Testaments of Francois Villon.

Translated by John Heron Lepper, including texts of John Payne and others. Liveright Publishing Corporation, 1924, Horace Liveright Inc., New York.

The Great Testament. Stanza XXVI, page 23.

3. Ballad that Villon made at the request of his mother, wherewithal to do her homage to our Lady . . .

> **Lady of Heaven, Regent of the earth,**
> **Empress of all the infernal marshes fell,**
> **Receive me, Thy poor Christian, 'spite my dearth,**
> **In the fair midst of Thine elect to dwell.**

A poor old wife I am, and little worth:

> **Nothing I know, nor letter aye could spell:**
> **Where in the church to worship I fare forth,**
> **I see Heaven limned, with harps and lutes, and Hell,**
> **Where damned folk seethe in fire unquenchable . . .**
> **Thou didst conceive, Princess most bright of sheen,**
> **Jesus the Lord, that hath nor end nor mean,**
> **Almighty, that, departing Heaven's demesne**
> **To succour us, put on our frailty,**
> **Offering to death His sweet of youth and green:**

Such as He is, our Lord He is, I ween!
In this belief I will to live and die.

The Complete Poems of Francois Villon / The Testaments of Francois Villon. Translated by John Heron Lepper, including the texts of John Payne and others. Horace Liveright Inc., Liveright Publishing Corporation, USA, 1924.

Supplement. *The Poems of Master Francois Villon of Paris*, first done into English verse, with a biographical and critical introduction by John Payne (The Villon Society, 1892).

The Greater Testament. Ballad that Villon made at the request of his mother, wherewithal to do her homage to Our Lady. Page 226-227. Stanzas I and III, Envoi.

Part 2. Scene 4.

     1. And had my life been still misspent,
       For such a sinner's punishment
       To burn to ashes were too good!
       'Tis need drives men to devilment
       And hunger wolves to leave the wood.

The Complete Poems of Francois Villon / The Testaments of Francois Villon. Translated by John Heron Lepper, including the texts of John Payne and others. Horace Liveright Inc., Liveright Publishing Corporation, USA, 1924.

The Great Testament. Stanza XXI, Page 22, line 4.

    2. Now here, now there, as the wind shifts its stead,
      We swing and creak and rattle overhead,

      No thimble dinted like our bird-pecked face.
      Brothers, have heed and shun the life we led:
      The rather pray, God grant us of His grace!

      Prince Jesus, over all empowered,
      Let us not fall into the Place of Dread,

But all our reckoning with the Fiend efface.
Folk, mock us not that are forspent and dead;
The rather pray, God grant us of His grace!

The Complete Poems of Francois Villon / The Testaments of Francois Villon. Translated by John Heron Lepper, including the texts of John Payne and others. Horace Liveright Inc., Liveright Publishing Corporation, USA, 1924.

Divers Poems. The Epitaph in ballad form that Villon made for himself and his companions, expecting no better than to be hanged in their company. Page 273, stanza III, starting from line 6.

Quotations Used in Parts 3 and 4

Part 3. Scene 1.

1. **I know all save myself alone**

   The Lyrics of Francois Villon. Printed for the members of the Limited Editions Club by the Spiral Press. Croton Falls, New York, 1933.

   Ballad of Things Known and Unknown. Translated by John Payne. Page 71, line 8.

2. **Most clement Prince, I'd have you be aware**
   That I'm like all, and yet apart and rare;
   Much understand, yet wit and knowledge shun:
   To have my wage again is all my care;
   Well entertained, rebuffed of every one.

   The Lyrics of Francois Villon. Printed for the members of the Limited Editions Club by the Spiral Press. Croton Falls, New York, 1933.

   Ballad written by Villon upon a subject proposed by Charles Duc D'Orleans. Translated by John Payne, page 66, line 5.

3. **But where are the snows of yester-year?**

   The Lyrics of Francois Villon. Printed for the members of the Limited Editions Club by the Spiral Press. Croton Falls, New York, 1933.

   Ballad of Dead Ladies. Translated by Dante Gabriel Rossetti. Page 23, line 8.

4.   All coins which wear thin of gold

The Lyrics of Francois Villon. Printed for the members of the Limited Editions Club by the Spiral Press. Croton Falls, New York, 1933.

Ballad and Creed of the Fair Armouress to the Daughters of Joy. Translated by Leonie Adams. Page 33, line 8.

1.   Even his fear of God would go . . . Happier he who says No!

The Lyrics of Francois Villon. Printed for the members of the Limited Editions Club by the Spiral Press. Croton Falls, New York, 1933.

Ballade of Good Advice. Translated by Leonie Adams. Page 34, stanza 3, lines 6 and 8.

Part 3. Scene 2.

1.   Had she, whom I have served of yore
So loyally with all my heart . . .
Had she but told me from the start
Her wishes, (Ah my vain regret!)
'Twould not have needed wizard's art
To draw back scatheless from her net.

Complete Poems of Francois Villon. The Testaments of Francois Villon. Translated by John Heron Lepper including the texts of John Payne and others. Liveright Publishing Corporation, New York, 1924.

The Great Testament, LV, pages 43-44.

2.   Honest liking is pretence, by rank falsehood truth is spread, and
only lovers have sound sense.

The Lyrical Poems of Francois Villon. The Limited Editions Club, New York, 1979.

Ballad of Contradictions. Translated by Leonie Adams. Page 63, stanza 2, line 6.

3. As I believe, she showed me favour
    With soft regrets and fine deceit
    To lend duplicity more savour
    And make my overthrow complete

    Full harsh and hard was her oppression;
    For she who cast a spell on me,
    Though I am guiltless of transgression,
    Has doomed me die, and her decree
    Is fixed that I shall cease to be.
    I find no safety but in flight.
    She means to break my life, I see,
    Nor will take pity on my plight.

Complete Poems of Francois Villon. The Testaments of Francois Villon.
Translated by John Heron Lepper including the texts of John Payne
and others. Liveright Publishing Corporation, New York, 1924.

The Little Testament. Page 4, stanza IV, lines 1-4, stanza V.

Part 3. Scene 3.

1. I laugh through tears, expect sans hope soe'er
    And comfort take amiddleward despair;
    Glad, though I joy in nought beneath the sun,
    Potent am I, and yet as weak as air;
    Well entertained, rebuffed of every one.

The Lyrics of Francois Villon. Printed for the members of the Limited
Editions Club by the Spiral Press, Croton Falls, New York, 1933.

Ballad written by Villon upon a subject proposed by Charles Duc
D'Orleans. Translated by John Payne. Page 64, stanza 1, lines 6-10.

Part 3. Scene 4.

1. Garnier, how like you my appeal?
    Did I wisely, or did I ill?
    Each beast looks to his own skin's weal:

... Long before this I should have swung,
A scarecrow hard by Montfaucon mill!
Was it a time to hold my tongue?

Complete Poems of Francois Villon. The Testaments of Francois Villon. Translated by John Heron Lepper including the texts of John Payne and others. Liveright Publishing Corporation, New York, 1924.

Divers Poems. Ballad of Villon's appeal. Page 275, stanza 1, lines 1-3, Envoi lines 2-4.

2. **Francois am I, woe worth is me! At Paris born, near Pontoise citie,**
    Whose neck, in the bight of a rope of three, Must prove how heavy
    my buttocks be.

The Lyrics of Francois Villon. Printed for the members of the Limited Editions Club by the Spiral Press, Croton Falls, New York, 1933.

The quatrain that Villon made when he was doomed to die. Translated by John Payne. Page 90.

3. **Joyeulx advenement! Joyeulx advenement!**

François Villon: A Documented Survey by D. B. Wyndham Lewis. The Literary Guild of America, J. J. Little & Ives Company, New York, 1928.

The Life, §6. Page 178.

4. **O blessed birth!**

Francois Villon: A Documented Survey by D. B. Wyndham Lewis. The Literary Guild of America, J. J. Little & Ives Company, New York, 1928.

The Life, §6. Page 168.

Part 4. Scene 1.

1. **How I regret my time of May,**
    My days of riot, now no more,

That unperceived stole away
Till age was knocking at the door.

Complete Poems of Francois Villon. The Testaments of Francois Villon.
Translated by John Heron Lepper including the texts of John Payne
and others. Liveright Publishing Corporation, New York, 1924.

The Great Testament. Page 22, stanza XXII, lines 1-4.

2. **A summer's tide on crusts I pined and water cold by his decree. He starved
    me sorely, harsh or kind. God be to him as he to me.**

Complete Poems of Francois Villon. The Testaments of Francois Villon.
Translated by John Heron Lepper including the texts of John Payne
and others. Liveright Publishing Corporation, New York, 1924.

The Great Testament. Page 16, stanza II, lines 5-8.

Part 4. Scene 2.

1. **Jenin l'Avenu,**
    Quick, while the baths are hot,
    Go, get a scrub, shoo!
    Jenin l'Avenu

The Lyrics of Francois Villon. Printed for the members of the Limited
Editions Club by the Spiral Press, Croton Falls, New York, 1933.

Jenin L'Avenu. Translated by Leonie Adams. Page 77, lines 1-4.

2. **Murder! Murder! They are killing me! I am dead!**

Francois Villon: A Documented Survey by D. B. Wyndham Lewis.
The Literary Guild of America, J. J. Little & Ives Company, New
York, 1928.

The Life, §8. Page 198. A letter of remission accorded by Louis XI,
dated November 1463.

Part 4. Scene 3.

1. **God knows I shall not dread the tomb**
    When all my merry times are flown

    Complete Poems of Francois Villon. The Testaments of Francois Villon.
    Translated by John Heron Lepper including the texts of John Payne
    and others. Liveright Publishing Corporation, New York, 1924.

    The Great Testament. Page 33, XLII, lines 7-8.

2. **Who did no wrong need not confess**

    Complete Poems of Francois Villon. The Testaments of Francois Villon.
    Translated by John Heron Lepper including the texts of John Payne
    and others. Liveright Publishing Corporation, New York, 1924.

    The Great Testament. Page 23, XXIV, line 8.

Part 4. Scene 4.

1. **Farewell, I say, with tearful eye**

    Complete Poems of Francois Villon. The Testaments of Francois Villon.
    Translated by John Heron Lepper including the texts of John Payne
    and others. Liveright Publishing Corporation, New York, 1924.

    Sundry Poems. Roundel. Page 286, line 1.

2. **The Court having considered the case brought by the provost**
    of Paris and his lieutenant against Master Francois Villon, and
    the latter having appealed from the sentence of hanging and
    strangling: It is finally ordered that the said appeal, and the
    sentence preceding, be annulled, and having regard to the bad
    character of the said Villon, that he be banished for ten years from
    the Town, Provosty, and Viscounty of Paris! Townspeople must
    not receive, comfort, nor aid in any way from the said Villon . . .

    Francois Villon: A Documented Survey by D. B. Wyndham Lewis. The
    Literary Guild of America, J. J. Little & Ives Company, New York,
    1928.

The Life, §8. Page 209, 211. The order of the Court of Parliament under the date of January 3, 1463.

3. **Farewell with heavy heart say I**

    Complete Poems of Francois Villon. The Testaments of Francois Villon. Translated by John Heron Lepper including the texts of John Payne and others. Liveright Publishing Corporation, New York, 1924.

    Sundry Poems. Roundel. Page 286, stanza 1, line 4.

4. **My princess, these resolves of mine ensure**
    My heart will never part from your heart, whether
    Come weal or woe: grant me a love as pure,
    E'en for this end we are alone together.

    Complete Poems of Francois Villon. The Testaments of Francois Villon. Translated by John Heron Lepper including the texts of John Payne and others. Liveright Publishing Corporation, New York, 1924.

    The Great Testament. Ballade that Villon gave to a gentleman newly married that he might send it to his wife won by his sword. Page 74, stanza 3, lines 9-12.

5. **Eternal rest be his for aye**
    In clear and everlasting light.

    Complete Poems of Francois Villon. The Testaments of Francois Villon. Translated by John Heron Lepper including the texts of John Payne and others. Liveright Publishing Corporation, New York, 1924.

    The Great Testament. Rondeau. Page 95.

2. **Repos eternel donne a cil,**
    Sire, et clarte perpetuelle.

    Francois Villon. Oeuvres. Editions Garnier Freres, Paris, 1962

    Le Testament. Epitaphe et Rondeau. Page 114, stanza 2, lines 1-2.

CPSIA information can be obtained at www.ICGtesting.com
Printed in the USA
LVOW091952070312

272065LV00001B/2/P